A Year Of Dominance

Peter Masters

Also by Peter Masters

The Control Book

Look Into My Eyes

Understanding BDSM Relationships

BDSM Relationships - How They Work

BDSM Relationships - Pitfalls and Obstacles

BDSM Relationships - Books 1, 2, and 3

This Curious Human Phenomenon

How to run BDSM workshops

Imperfect Journeys

ISBN 978-0-9923263-2-6

Cover art by Peter Masters
http://www.peter-masters.com/

Contents

Week 1

Being a sadist

The topics of sadism, masochism and sadomasochism arise frequently in our BDSM world. Indeed, BDSM, by definition (the "SM" bit in the acronym), is about sadism and masochism.

My dictionary defines sadism as "the tendency to derive pleasure, especially sexual gratification, from inflicting pain, suffering, or humiliation on others."

I think that there's an important disconnect here between What It Is That We Do (WIITWD) and sadism (or masochism).

A number of times in my various writings over the years I've said that people don't look for pain *per se*, but instead they look for where pain takes them, or they look for the result of pain, or they look for their reaction to pain. They don't just look for pain and then it all stops once they've said, "Ouch."

I've had a number of discussions with people about this and once, when I had this written prominently on the main page of my website, I had a stranger write to me and earnestly berate me because, he claimed, he and his friends just looked for pain. I think he was wrong.

Pain hurts. That's what it is designed (in the Mother Nature-sense) to do. It's not meant to be nice and I argue that it never is.

But pain can lead to good things. It can be educational, as in "That was a bad idea and I won't be trying that again". Or one of the current drums I beat is that pain also has the ability to push away the rational parts of our minds and expose the primal parts and give them a very good airing. This outcome is, I think, a very good thing. In fact, I think it is a very, very desirable thing.

However, pain was not the destination in either of the two examples in the previous paragraph. It was the way to get to the destination, but not the destination itself.

My point is that when we consider the idea of "Why BDSM equals sadism" and think in terms of pain, we're missing something important. Pain is not the end game.

We sometimes use pain to get to that end game, but not always.

If we consider ourselves as sadists because we "get pleasure out of inflicting pain" then I'd argue that we're not seeing the whole picture. For example, if I were to say that I use pain to help my girl find surrender, enlightenment and discover herself and I am very happy when she does, then no one would call that sadistic.

If I were to say that I use pain to help my girl uncover her primal core and have Earth-shaking orgasms that would make even Vesuvius feel ashamed, then no one would call that sadistic either.

But if I leave out the bit about the outcome and just say, I like inflicting pain on my girl, then it really does sound sadistic and I am doing a disservice to myself, my goals and my girl.

2

And I think if we talk about us being sadists, then I think we're doing the same. We're minimising what we do. We don't just hit someone so that they go, "Ouch."

Which leads me to say: I am not a sadist.

I am, however, very interested in personal growth, enlightenment, satisfaction, education, self-actualisation and empowerment. If pain forms part of the road to get there, then I think it's just as valid as training, discipline, bondage or whatever.

Week 2

Fully-informed surrender

I like the submissives and slaves in my life to be knowledgeable. Well..., to be honest, I like everyone in my life to be knowledgeable, but I'm writing about BDSM here and BDSM-wise the people I like to hang around with are submissives and slaves (preferably young, fit and female, with big boobs, but I'm a guy so shoot me, but that's a separate topic).

Anyway, when I say knowledgeable, I don't just mean having technical knowledge or skills, but being knowledgeable and aware about what's happening between them and me, and particularly what's happening inside them. I want them to understand submission and slavery. I want them to know surrender, to feel it, to recognise it, to not be afraid of it.

I am, in fact, looking for fully-informed surrender.

Which, of course, means that I prefer an informed partner. One who chooses to stay ignorant is one who I quickly scrub from my list. Instead, one who chooses to learn, one who asks questions, whose need to learn burns deep inside her, she is the one I hunger to explore, dominate and control.

I long ago gave up the idea of trying to be an amazing man of mystery. For a brief time when I was young it used to be exciting when a fine female would put me on a pedestal and think I was awesome. My ego loved it, but it disconnected me from these women. It created distance.

Instead, I want these females to know the real place I have in their surrender. I am just a dude - a dude who writes, who is knowledgeable, who has done interesting things, who has faced interesting challenges, and who himself strives to learn. I want my place in the lives of these females to be due to the real me, not a fantasy me or a me-on-a-pedestal.

For that reason I deliberately make an effort NOT to be a man of mystery. I don't keep secrets. I don't try to keep submissives or slaves in the dark. If they ask something, I answer. Even if they don't ask, I'm quite likely to explain. I don't want their surrender because of ignorance. I want..., or better said, I need their fully-informed surrender because then I know that it's really me who is a part of it. Then it is intense. Then it is personal and intimate.

I try to present myself as I am. For example, I freely admit that I am particular bad at bondage. Knots stay in place as long as my partner doesn't move, stretch, twitch or breath. If they do any of these, the ropes fall off. I don't know why. They just do.

I've found that saying, "I don't know," can be one of the most powerful things. It often directs my own explorations when I'm writing. I try to share, even to teach, through my books and articles. When I'm trying to explain something, to connect some ideas so that they make sense, I might reach a gap and realise that I can't connect idea A to idea C because *I don't know* idea B and need to find it. It's like a join-the-dots drawing where you have to provide some of the dots yourself.

"I don't know" is also a powerful thing to say to a submissive or slave when they ask something. I'd argue that a submissive or slave who is fully-aware of their dominant's or master's shortcomings as much as his strengths is going to surrender more, not less.

And, in fact, this is the reality I'm looking for. This is the surrender I'm looking for. One based on knowing, on awareness, on no secrets, and on no ignorance.

Week 3

Enslavement

One of the more interesting and ego-deflating things I have learned about BDSM is that masters don't enslave slaves. Slaves, in fact, enslave themselves. Yes, it's not me or my amazing awesomeness that reduces a woman into a quivering, subservient creature. She does it herself.

However, that's not to say that a master doesn't have a necessary role.

Let me explain because this is important.

Someone doesn't just become slave because a dude in tight leathers or a chick in black latex appears on the horizon. In most, if not all cases, the slave is sitting inside them, waiting to come out, waiting for the right time, the right circumstances and the right master or mistress.

Why doesn't the slave come out before then? There are many reasons. It might be that the person who is slave is distracted by other activities which are partially satisfying their slave needs - for example, if they have a a deep need to serve they might work for a charity and sublimate some of their need to serve through that. It might also be that each time they find someone who they feel could be "the one", it turns out that they are, in fact, "the dud" and their slave part goes into hiding. For many slaves, they may not even realise they are slaves because their slave nature or condition can't find a safe way to come out and subconsciously they keep it bottled up.

Enter the master...

Regardless of the nature of a slave, a key part of being slave is surrender. They need to surrender completely to what they are. They will seek surrender, but partial surrender will always be unsatisfying, even painful and torturous, and some slaves, in their hunger and desperation, will take partial surrender as better than nothing at all.

The right master, however, can provide two things:

1. They can provide a safe context for the slave to come out, and

2. They can provide the right opportunities for service and surrender.

It can be the case that the slave stays bottled up because coming out is painful, because they get abused, because they aren't respected or appreciated, or even because they get belittled. A right master will recognised what's happening. They'll remove obstacles and impediments, get rid of the things which keep the slave bottled up inside themselves, and create situations where the slave's nature can be fully and safely exposed. Someone who is slave is going to always a feel a pressure to be themselves, so when all obstacles are removed the slave will tend to come out naturally.

Secondly, a slave just isn't slave on their own. Well... they are, but it's when they're paired with a master who knows how to use them, who knows what to demand of them, and knows how to treat them, that the slave can be all that they need to be. Certainly a slave can pair up with someone who doesn't fully understand them and can be of service to this person and sate some of their slave needs that way, but an aware master can bring everything into sharp focus and make being slave challenging, demanding, and deeply satisfying.

So, the goal is not to find the slave. The slave is already there. The goal is to let the slave be born and to provide the nourishment the slave needs to grow. If you can also teach, more the better. But remember that the goal of a teacher or trainer is not to make the slave into what you want, but to make the slave into all they can be.

Week 4

Three submissives walk into a bar...

In the last couple of years I've done two kinky humour projects. One was a book, the other an online web course[1]. After thinking about humour a lot I have made an interesting observation: Humour and kink don't go together. That's not to say that us kinky folk can't be funny, but funny is not something we really look to introduce into our activities.

Now, I should mention for those who have only just tuned in, that as far as kink is concerned I have two areas of interest. One is erotic hypnosis. Actually, "erotic hypnosis" is the politically correct name for it. Because we're all grown-ups here, I think that I could say that it's simply another way to getting into someone's pants, this time involving hypnotising them first. It

---

[1]The book is "Imperfect Journeys". The web course is "Looking at naked ladies" which can be found at http://www.bdsmworkbook.com/

can be exceptional in terms of pants-entry-success-percentage and frequently seems to work better than asking, "Do you like rope?"

My second kinky interest is BDSM.

I have a good sense of humour. Even my dentist says so and a dental surgery is not the place where you'd expect to get many laughs. I also have what could be called eclectic tastes in humour and I like Futurama, Robot Chicken, the Marx Brothers and - on the other side of the pond - Morecambe and Wise, The Goons and Monty Python.

But, to my frequent frustration, I can't really combine humour and kinkiness. I have learned that the times when either erotic hypnosis or BDSM are happening are not the times for humour.

There are good reasons why this is so.

BDSM is often at its best when we're totally focussed on it. As a master I get the most bang for my buck when I'm totally engrossed in the shared experience. Humour, on the other hand, is often a relief valve, a way of releasing tension. That's not what I'm looking for in BDSM. Well, not often, anyway. I don't want the tension or expectation to be suddenly diffused through a witty remark about, say, hamsters. Instead, I want the focus to remain tight and intense both for me and my partner.

Additionally, one of the consequences of sub-space is a state of mind which doesn't appreciate humour. I can't remember which book I wrote it in, but I've written that you don't find chess boards or Scrabble™ sets in BDSM dungeons. The states of mind we look for in BDSM are not Scrabble- or chess-compatible. They're not humour-compatible either. We're looking for something primal, not rational or intellectual. While picture books with photographs of fine-figured females in rope-assisted contortions with extraordinary objects impossibly inserted in various orifices

14

are often welcome additions to a dungeon, collections of the Wizard of Id, Charlie Brown or Garfield are not. They don't help achieve a suitable state of mind.

In the hypnosis arena, someone who is deeply hypnotised isn't going to laugh at a joke - they're hypnotised after all. Rather than spend the time crafting some masterful witticism, you can get a much bigger laugh from them by simply telling them that they've just seen something very funny.

For someone like me with a sense of humour that sometimes just aches to get out, BDSM and erotic hypnosis can be places of strangely perverted frustrations and delights. There can be intense excitement, challenge and joy in each but, sadly, no bad puns.

Beforehand and, er, afterhand we can joke around and tease, but during scenes when the profound is at stake it's appropriate to remain serious.

I thought that before I wrap up this little essay, I'd share with you some jokes.

As far as jokes go, hypnosis is very poorly represented. The only hypnosis joke I've every heard or read goes basically as follows.

> A stage hypnotist hypnotises a group of people. Once they're under and he's ready to start the main part of his show, a bee lands on him and stings him. In a loud voice he yells, "Shit!" It takes weeks to clean up the theatre.

On the other hand, there seem to be many more BDSM-related jokes.

> Q. Why does a man start panting, go weak at the knees and act crazy when a woman wears a leather dress?

A. Because she smells like a new truck.

Q. What's green and carries a whip?

A. Kermit the Flog

Two women meet for the first time after high school. As they discuss what they do now, their husbands, kids, their sex lives, etc., one happens to mention S&M.

The other is surprised, "Why, Jenny! I never thought you were the type for that."

Jenny replies, "Why, sure. While Roger snores, I masturbate."

One day a woman was cleaning her son's bedroom and found an S&M magazine. When her husband came home that night she showed it to him and asked what they should do about it. The husband replied, "Well, I certainly don't think we should spank him!"

Week 5

Performance of dominants

Many, if not all dominants, masters and mistresses are familiar with an expectation to perform. This is particularly the case when there's a strong physical component to the relationship they have with their submissive or slave.

After all, a submissive or slave signs up to be with a dominant or master because they have a need or desire they want met. There's sort of an implicit understanding that this is actually going to happen and that the submissive's needs will be satisfied.

You can't just satisfy a submissive once however. In any sort of ongoing relationship the dominant needs to do it over and over again. Their submissive, on the other hand, might just need to take off their clothes, do what they're told and be receptive.

OK. So I'm deliberately trying to make this sound one-sided here. What I'm trying to get at is that dominants and masters are the ones who nominally have the authority to make the decisions. It can feel like a lonely place and this "burden of command" can be something they experience very strongly.

This can end up creating a type of performance anxiety. I'm not talking about not being able to get one's end up, but instead I'm talking about the possible doubts about being able to sustain the dominance, maintain the passion for the rope, be demanding in calls for service, and basically bring out on demand the power which both they and their submissive need and hunger for.

I suggested above that this can have to do with physical BDSM, but it's not just confined to dungeons, rope, floggers, riding crops and nipple clamps. Any time that the dominant needs to be in charge, make decisions, or be a pillar of authority they can feel this pressure.

This expectation to perform, and its sometimes concomitant fear of not being able to, is typically self-induced. Of course it shouldn't be this way.

Particularly for the dominant, but also for the submissive, it's important to remember that all of this dominant/submissive and master/slave stuff is a team effort and that each member of the team is human and mortal. The teams are usually teams of two. And the two people involved are not playing against each other. They're on the same side.

It might be that the dominant is the team captain, but the submissive is not just there as decoration or as muscle. They have a mind, feelings and their own experiences. In some cases they can even be more experienced than their master. They do contribute and, importantly, this means that their dominant or master is not alone. Dominants, keep this in mind.

The pressure to perform which the dominant can experience can come from a number of places. I'll mention just two of them here.

The first is a desire to make a good impression with a new partner. This is, of course, not unique to BDSM.

18

The second has to do with a mistaken idea, typically associated with ego, that the dominant is Superman.

As to the first, what you're there for, and what your submissive is there for, is so that you can be dominant. If something hasn't worked out, or if you're not feeling well, or if you just aren't in the mood, take charge of the situation. Don't force yourself to do something. If you force yourself to engage your submissive and the appropriate juices aren't flowing then it won't feel right and it especially won't be as satisfying for either of you than it would be if you waited for the right time.

As a dominant, don't expect to be able to be dominant all the time. Sometimes it doesn't happen. Sometimes the dominant thing to do is to make an executive decision and go out and have a coffee instead.

Secondly, being a dominant often has to do with control, and if ego is controlling you and making you try to be a dominant when you're sick, tired or just not in the mood, then you're not really in control. In fact, with your ego in control combined with a need to perform, you might just end up being completely sucked dry. It has happened many, many times before to greater supermen than you.

On the other hand, if you've spent the last two weeks building up your submissive's expectations for tonight, teasing them and taunting them, and working them up into a lather of anticipation, and then when they knock on the door you tell them that you've changed your mind and are just taking them out for tea and scones at the local all-night cafe, then you deserve everything that's coming to you.

20

Week 6

Where is the mastery?

There's a very big difference between the reality of BDSM and the ideas which "vanilla" or "white bread" folk have about BDSM. I think that most of this difference is due to the lack of realistic depictions of BDSM relationships and activities in any sort of media. As a result, fantasists are more-or-less free to weave incredible stories and ideas about BDSM without much risk of being corrected. These stories tell of worlds which are far superior, far more arousing, far more fantastic and often far more one-dimensional than any sort of actuality. Consider, for example, the people who show up on the Internet doorsteps of dominatrices claiming to be slaves and who beg and plead to be locked in a cage for the rest of their lives, or those who have never been flogged before but claim to be ready to submit to a long, hard and extreme flogging. Clearly, to us anyway, they're living outside of reality and if anyone actually gave them what they're asking for they'd be extremely "disappointed" with the result.

Keeping that bit of background in mind, I wanted to mention that I was perusing the interwebs the other day and came across a discussion on a BDSM site which was about women who refuse to give blowjobs. The comments - from guys, of course - started out like this:

"All my females suck cock or else they're whipped, raped and face-fucked by me!"

"Women who don't give blowjobs are worthless property."

"Females who don't fulfil their purpose should be traded in just like a car that doesn't run any more."

"All holes or nothing!"

Now admittedly the group in which this discussion was taking place was called, "Women are property of men", but I can't help wondering, where is the mastery here? Is there reality here?

I'm physically quite strong and I'm sure I could force a woman to yield to my desires. My first book was about hypnosis and sex and with my knowledge and experience I'm sure many females would succumb to my spell and "all holes" would become available. I have also written a number of books on BDSM and I'm sure I could use this fact to bluff or intimidate an innocent or unwary female into giving me what I want. But are any of these mastery?

I think not.

Now I know that rough-handling works for many slaves and for many submissives some of the time. As a dominant it works some of the time for me too. But mastery is more than rough-handling. It's certainly much more than finessing your way into any of a woman's orifices.

What I'm saying is that people have been trying to get into the pants (or mouths) of other people for time immemorial. Mastery is more than conning your way in, intimidating or manipulating your way in, forcing your way in, or even just demanding your way in.

For me, it's about actively playing a part in creating a context, state of mind or mindset in your slave or submissive where the clear, obvious and often only choice is to present that hole for you to use.

And, of course, it's not just about holes.

Week 7

The Voice

When I was learning hypnosis and hypnotherapy, one of the very important parts of that was developing The Voice. Basically, The Voice is a way of talking you adopt when you mean business as opposed to the rest of the time.

What I mean is that when you have someone you hypnotise on a regular basis, whether it is someone you hypnotise as part of therapy they are undergoing with you, or whether it is someone else who you hypnotise for pleasure such as for recreational erotic hypnosis, the fact is that they are going to become used to being hypnotised by you and might "pop off" into a trance when you don't really want them to.

While it might sound as though hypnotherapy is always about hypnosis, there are times you want your client in a trance and times when you don't, such as when you're arranging their next session, when you're discussing their bill, or if you have to ring them up to reschedule an appointment.

To prevent unplanned trances, many hypnotists and hypnotherapists develop The Voice. It's a different set of verbal habits and intonations which we use when actually hypnotising someone compared to the way we speak the rest of the time. The Voice is usually deeper, more insistent and slightly slower than normal. By switching into The Voice we often don't need to actually do much hypnotising with regular clients or subjects because once they hear The Voice they're mostly "gone" straight away.

BDSM also has The Voice. Or, more precisely, many dominants and masters have The Voice. It's the way they speak to their slave or submissive when they mean business. In other words, when they're focussed and intent. And, for exactly the same reasons why hypnotherapists develop The Voice, masters and dominants should all develop it, too. If you're a submissive or slave reading this and you've been around the block a few times, you can probably think of a few masters and mistresses from your past who used The Voice, who had a very different way of talking to you when they meant business compared to when they were simply chilling out.

Developing The Voice helps dominants and masters in a couple of ways.

Firstly, just like in hypnosis and when you're with an experienced subject, The Voice acts like a trigger. It puts your slave or submissive instantly in a responsive state of mind. Even without telling them to do anything, by adopting The Voice you'll find they're suddenly sitting up straighter and are keenly focussed on you. If they're trained in different protocols, The Voice will immediately shift them into a higher one. It gets their attention.

Secondly, The Voice prevents miscommunication and confusion. If you like teasing your submissive or joking around sometimes, then you can do that to your heart's content in your normal voice and they'll know exactly what's going on. But when you switch into The Voice they'll know immediately that there are no more jokes and it's time to be very serious.

For those dominants and masters reading this, The Voice is an extremely useful tool. If you haven't done so already, it's worth devoting time to it. Try to think about how you sound to your slave or submissive at different times. Think about what you're feeling and how it's reflected in what you say and especially in how you say it. The Voice is typically calm and determined. It carries authority. It's definitely not high or shrill.

And, of course, then there's The Look, but we'll leave that for another day...

Week 8

Learning curve

There's no doubt that there's a bit of a learning curve involved in BDSM. I'm not talking about the physical side of BDSM here, though it's true that learning how to flog or be flogged, or tie or be tied, have their own challenges and can take considerable time to... um, master. No, what I'm talking about is what we have to learn about ourselves.

For many of us, BDSM is quite unlike anything we've done before and it can be very difficult to work out where we belong or how we fit in. Someone who enters the world of BDSM convinced that their place is as a dominant might easily discover a couple of years later that they really are better suited to being a slave.

We might attribute this relatively sudden switching from one role to its opposite to personal growth, but can personal growth account for this, and so quickly? I wonder if it can. I wonder if it's not something else.

Many people get into BDSM because of deep wants or needs which they can't meet elsewhere.

But what happened before they discovered BDSM? If they have wants or needs which are best met in a BDSM relationship such as dominance and submission, or through some BDSM activity such as flogging, how did they manage?

The answer is that they sublimated, which basically means they made do with what was available.

Of course, making do is not always enough. "Making do" is typically the poor cousin to profound satisfaction.

A problem here is that before we discover BDSM, "vanilla" life gives us tantalising hints of what might be. A particularly shapely and keen-to-serve shop assistant can stir things up for dominants [Is my heterosexuality leaking out here?] and a strong authority figure can stir things up for submissives. The hunger is awoken and brought into focus but there isn't anything to really satisfy it.

When we do come face to face with BDSM, say through a partner willing to experiment or by encountering "the scene", it can be a bit like a kid in a candy shop. Things inside us, the wants and needs which have never been fully or properly met, can suddenly burst out like, "Hey! Hey! Hey! It's party time!"

Here, even some strange dude with a pair of fluffy handcuffs, or someone who's happy to kneel for a bit with their clothes off, can be the most exciting thing since sliced bread.

Can you remember your first BDSM explorations? Were they exciting? Were they as sophisticated back then as they are now? Are you even still on the same "side" now as you were then?

Once we make any sort of commitment to BDSM the floggings occur more often, the chances to serve are more frequent, the kneeling becomes more serious and we quickly move beyond the fluffy handcuff stage. Instead of experiencing unsatisfied hunger, we become used to being "fed". At the same time, this freedom from hunger lets us begin to look deeper into what we really need because we're no longer distracted by the hunger.

We start looking for something more refined. And each time we find it, we start looking for something even more refined.

And I think that word: "refined", is the key to this.

I suspect that the changes in what we look for BDSM-wise are a matter of our personal taste becoming more refined. Or, perhaps I should say that we uncover what our tastes are. And I think it's an iterative process, one which we need to keep repeating as we discover each new layer.

We don't really learn that much about BDSM. Instead we learn about ourselves.

But maybe this is personal growth. Maybe it's not so much about changing, but about uncovering and discovering what's already there.

Week 9

People skills, people!

I was at a meeting recently where a couple of the folk suggested that someone young and without much experience can't really be a master. I both agree and disagree with this.

If we're talking about skill then I agree. It takes years to gain the variety of experience with a wide range of submissives and slaves as well as the variety of experience with a wide range of BDSM practices and techniques to be a BDSM master in a technical sense.

On the other hand, someone who has a profound relationships with a slave, who finds deep satisfaction with a slave, who can bring out the best in the slave, and who can put the slave to full use, is someone I'd readily call a master. They might never master anyone else in their life beyond this single slave, but when they are the master in even just one fully-functional master/slave relationship then I'd have no hesitation in according them the title.

I say this because, ultimately, I don't think there's much point in measuring up someone for masterhood by just looking at their skills with a rope, how well they can do suspension bondage, their ability at needle play, or how hard and for long they can deliver a wallop. All these count for nothing if the master can't master a slave or a submissive.

It's admirable to aspire to greatness with knots or with impact play, but the end goal for a master will always be the effective engagement of a slave or a submissive. Everything else comes second. We should never lose sight of this.

I write this because it is diabolically easy to fall into the trap of focussing too much on the mechanical skills side of BDSM and not enough on the people skills side. This actually applies just as much to submissive and slaves as it does to dominants and masters, but it is sometimes more obvious in the latter because people skills are hard and when there are difficulties in a relationship it can be remarkably tempting to think that more or harder floggings, or more or tighter bondage is the answer.

So, extending what I wrote just two paragraphs ago about the measure of mastery being effective engagement of a slave or a submissive, what we should look for in BDSM generally is not so much the collection or perfection of mechanical skills, but more how we engage and affect our partners.

People skills, people! That's what it's about.

Week 10

Consent of a comedian

I am not some super master.

I write this because there seems to be some expectation that I am a switched-on, 24-hour-a-day, take-on-all-comers dude ready to impose my mighty will on any submissive or slave who is ready for some D&s action.

It's true that I have written some books on the subjects of both BDSM and of getting my wicked way with females. I can even stare most intently and in a fashion which can send a female scurrying for replacement underwear.

I don't do it all the time though. I sometimes like time off.

There is understandable outrage when a master or dominant does something to a slave or a submissive without their consent or when they use their masterly wiles to trigger some sort of involuntary or unwelcome reaction in a submissive. But equally unreasonable is the slave or submissive who does the same to a master. For example, bowing or kneeling at the feet of a master who is not your own, while flattering and exciting, can also be unwelcome.

Us masters are simply mere mortals and trying to get a masterly rise out of us can sometimes be successful even when we have the most serious intention of remaining aloof and distant in that annoying way we have. Just because we respond doesn't mean that there's consent involved.

I'm reminded of the comedians we see on stage and TV. They may be just as funny off stage as they are on stage, but expecting them to be funny and ready to tell a joke when they're not on stage is an imposition. It's non-consensual. When they're on stage and we look for them to tell us a joke, that's probably quite reasonable. Off stage though, it's not reasonable. There is no implied or explicit contract which says they should be funny to our timetable. And just because they might be chronically funny and unable to stop themselves, or because they feel obligated or because they don't want to disappoint doesn't mean we should take advantage of them.

Ditto for masters and dominants.

Unless we're talking about that breed of dominant known as a "service dominant", we don't expect to hear things from a submissive like, "Oh, look. It's 5pm. Time for my afternoon submission. Master Kenneth, come here. I need you!"

Masters and dominants actually need time off. We like to watch the TV sometimes without feeling obliged to use our submissive as a footrest. It can be good when our submissives or slaves can fetch us a drink without us needing to put on dominant airs and thanking them in our most grave voices thus sending shivers down to their groins or elsewhere.

There are, of course, strategies we masters can use to prevent unwanted advances or to discourage untimely submission from others. My favourite is to wear a Hawaiian shirt and shorts, possibly with a few dabs of obvious sunscreen if I'm outdoors.

36

Ultimately though, it's a matter of consent. Submissives and slaves may not realise that they're looking for mastery or domination outside of the bounds of comfort, need, or desire of the master or dominant. It's important for us masters and dominants to recognise when it happens. It can be subtle. It can be just a niggly feeling of not being quite comfortable with what's going on, or it can something major like, "What's this naked person doing in my bedroom!?!?"

A good question to ask yourself at these times is: Is this what I signed up for?

Week 11

Wherefore art thou, BDSM?

The experience of BDSM can be quite intense, even intoxicating. This intensity can make it something highly desirable.

However, seeing a relationship or a partner through eyes coloured by lust, hunger or passion can give you a distorted view. What can seem to be shared can be one-sided, what might seem to be dominance can be lust drive, and what might seem to be submission can be sensation hunger.

On top of this, if all you have ever felt or encountered is a hunger for sensation, then it can be very easy to think that this is all there is in BDSM. You can call yourself a submissive and be utterly convinced that what you experience is the peak of BDSM, the end all, the top of the mountain, and that there is nowhere higher to go.

Likewise, a dominant who has a few miles on the clock in the flogging and bondage departments may see these two activities as the epitome of BDSM, that he (or she) is at the top of their particular heap because of their obvious skill and prowess, and that they are a master because have learned all there is about the things they are aware of or because they have had a few subbies crawling at their feet.

This is understandable to a certain extent because of the often hidden and mysterious nature of BDSM. That's not to say that BDSM is particularly mysterious in itself, but there are many aspects of BDSM which you simply won't encounter unless you are well-travelled, have lots of experience, and have a certain amount of luck.

If you and your partner are absolutely happy and content with what you do, then exploring further afield is unnecessary and maybe even a waste of time.

If, however, you take someone under your wing to teach them, then I think it behooves you to make sure that you aren't teaching them a limited view which, while OK for you, may not be OK for them. If they look up to you then they may not realise that there's more to BDSM. They may not think to look further because you yourself do not.

So, if your partner or your local community looks up to you as a father figure, mother figure, guiding light or leather-clad angel, then do consider attending the occasional workshop, joining the occasional discussion group, and generally broadening your horizons. Even if what you see and learn by doing this isn't useful for you personally, you've put yourself in a position where you can at least give pointers to others who take inspiration from you.

Week 12

When the slave is ready...

I saw someone take the old saying, "When the student is ready the teacher will appear," and adapt it to BDSM by saying, "When the slave is ready, the master will appear."

I think that the "student" which the first saying is talking about is a student of life, so can we compare a student of life to a slave? I'm sure that a slave can be a student of life but does a master then fill some role which we can compare to a teacher. I suppose they sometimes do because a lesson can be learned from anyone, anyone at all. But, if we're actually talking about a slave rather than a student, can we expect a right master to appear when the slave is ready?

Indeed, what does *ready* mean for a slave?

I think that there are two stages to being *ready*.

The first is recognising that there is a need, desire or a hunger waiting to be satisfied. Once recognised, a slave might go looking for a master, a dominant might go looking for a submissive, or a student might go looking for a teacher.

There's a good chance that even when they know that they need something they won't be able to find it. No teacher will seem to have the answers the student needs, every master the slave meets will only provide cursory comfort, and every submissive the dominant encounters will only seem to be able to satisfy part of their particular need.

Does this sound like a familiar situation?

Often, the problem is that the person who feels the need is trying to conquer it, to put themselves in the driver's seat and bring satisfaction to themselves directly.

Much of the time this doesn't work. The reason will become apparent shortly.

Thus entereth the second stage of being ready.

The second stage involves surrender. It involves recognising that you can't be both in the driver's seat and get what you need at the same time. Many people keep trying however. They butt their head against this wall which is blocking them from getting their needs met for their whole lives and can't work out what's wrong.

If you're looking for a slave, or a submissive, or a dominant, or a master who dresses a particular way, or who talks a particular way, or who does particular things with or to you, then you're going to be waiting a very long time.

It may well be that there's someone right for you, but they might look and act nothing like what you have in mind. Whatever rules or ideas you have about getting what you need, abandon them. Get out of the driver's seat and give up on the idea of you deciding what the right person needs to be. You might not recognise the right master for you, the right slave for you, even the right teacher for you until you accept that they're not going to appear in the form you want. They're not going to behave how you want.

Learning this, surrendering to this, brings you closer to being *ready*. The first stage of *ready* is merely recognising the need. The second stage is accepting that what's important are the need's own terms, not yours.

When you recognise, when you accept deep down, that you can't decide what satisfies you, that you can't choose what completes you or what makes you whole, then, and only then, are you *ready*.

Week 13

Vulnerability

One of the ideas I have been exploring in my writing over the last few years is that of penetration - namely the importance of being able to affect and be affected (i.e., penetrated) by our BDSM partners.

While it's probably quite apparent that a top needs to be able to affect their bottom such as by causing them to jump, cry out in agony, or be completely unable to move or speak, and that a dominant needs to be able to affect or control their submissive through orders or by putting them to use, it's less obvious that this ability or openness to being affected must work both ways.

It has long been possible to automate many typical BDSM activities. Whipping and caning, for example, are simple mechanical actions easily amenable to being performed indefatigably by a machine, yet we never see such machines at parties or see them advertised in magazines when, at first thought, these would seem ideal for pain sluts and discipline aficionados.

Likewise, why should a top be burdened by needing to tie up a real person when a life-sized, plastic mannequin would do just as well?

A mannequin wouldn't be subject to cramps and wouldn't need to be monitored to make sure they are OK healthwise.

We actually have real, flesh-and-blood partners because we need to experience them and their reactions to us. Without a flesh-and-blood partner and without their responses any BDSM activity seems hollow. The more we are affected by our partner, the more intense the experience is for us.

Interestingly, it is often this readiness to be affected which determines whether someone - dominant or submissive, top or bottom - is in it for a relationship with a partner or is in it just for some quick jollies.

Another word for describing readiness to be affected is vulnerability.

We are all vulnerable to some extent. Some people choose to protect themselves from pain and hurt by building a wall around themselves. A wall, however, does not discriminate - it will protect you just as much from good times and good experiences as it will protect you from bad times and bad experiences. The only way to make sure that you fully receive the benefits of the many opportunities, relationships and experiences which come your way is not to block them with a wall or to filter them in some way. It is to be as open to as many things as possible, to accept that sometimes there will be duds and that there will sometimes be fleeting hurt.

If you build up your internal strength then you can suffer the slings and arrows of outrageous fortune[1] with only the risk of occasional hurt and still be open to the deepest and most satisfying shared experiences with your partner or partners.

---

[1]Thanks, William Shakespeare!

Building up this strength involves deliberately letting down your walls and exposing yourself. It takes time and persistence. Indeed, it can be very hard, as The Bible says, "to turn the other cheek" after being hurt, or to get back on that horse straight after falling off, but this is the way it is done.

It is worth reflecting on your own walls. Regardless of whether you are a master or a slave, a dominant or a submissive, a top or a bottom, what walls do you have? What purpose do your walls serve? And what are they really protecting you from?

Week 14

Reflections on service

I am a service-oriented dominant. That is to say that I like receiving service. Offer to give me a good backscratching or to fetch me a chocolate biscuit (Arnott's Mint Slices preferred) and I'm all yours.

Many years ago I went to a BDSM party in the company of a fine, submissive female with whom I was well acquainted. What we negotiated beforehand was that she would be attending me for the duration of the party. I had visions of good company, ready obedience, immediate availability, intelligent conversation and more.

Early on during the party, and while I was watching another couple intently involved in some rope-and-leather-action, I sent my submissive-of-the-evening to fetch me a drink.

And I waited.

And I waited.

And she didn't come back. So I went to find her.

When I found her, she was standing, with my slowly-warming drink in her hand, talking to two of her friends.

I was initially puzzled about why she did this, but it was here that I got my first inkling that there are at least two different types of service:

1. Reciprocal service, and

2. Self-sacrificing service.

It occurred to me that my role at this particular party was that I was actually supposed to be serving my submissive-of-the-evening. I was involved in a reciprocal service deal. This hadn't dawned on me earlier. Even though it hadn't been discussed or agreed, my implicit role was that I would be her dominant for the evening and that I would, at the very least, do "things" so that she could feel submissive. In return, she would bring me drinks which were still cold, delight me with enchanting conversation rather than talk to other people and so on. When I reflected on this I realised that I hadn't been doing "things" and she had probably experienced the equivalent of subbie boredom or subbie restlessness.

For this type of submissive service is reciprocal - a sort of barter arrangement. If I want a backscratching, then she'd be wanting the equivalent of having her back scratched in return. When my service to her deteriorated, so did hers to me.

On the other hand, there are some submissives and slaves who get all the reward, pleasure and satisfaction they need simply from the service itself. These are self-sacrificing folk - it is the act of giving that is their reward. The more they give of themselves the better they feel. The role of the dominant or master is very different here. It is to ensure that there are opportunities where the submissive can

50

serve and know that their service is useful, valued and appreciated. This isn't just make-work. It isn't just trying to think of things to keep the submissive busy. It needs to be valuable.

I think that we could argue about whether my party submissive was a bottom, a submissive, a slave or something else, but an important point is that bottoms, submissives and slaves of all flavours are never there to simply give, regardless of whether we're talking about reciprocal service, self-sacrificing service, or some other type of service. There has to be something they take from it. There always has to be some positive outcome for them.

Importantly, they - like many dominants - don't always know what they need and oftentimes might only realise that something is missing. This realisation might not even be conscious. It might be their unconscious mind which responds to the lack of whatever-it-is: pain, surrender, duties, discipline, whatever. The acting out we sometimes see can actually be their unconscious mind trying to provoke us to give it what they need.

Dominants, too, can get into this situation where everything looks OK between them and their submissive, but at the same time something still feels missing.

When we set up shop with a D&s partner, even if just temporarily, there's an implicit expectation on both sides that needs will be met as a result of this pairing. While we often might negotiate beforehand what each of us is going to physically do, we don't always say which wants and needs we are actually trying to satisfy. In the case of me and my party submissive, this is something I neglected to ask, and in the absence of her telling me I should have made the effort to find out.

When we receive service from a household domestic we know that they get paid a salary and probably get some measure of pleasure from doing their job well. When we have a submissive or slave serving us, what do they need? They don't get a salary. What is it that they look for, consciously or unconsciously, which motivates them to serve? If they don't consciously know the answer themselves, how can we work it out?

My takeaway from this is that even with the best will and intentions in the world we aren't always going to find out from our partners everything that they need from us, and they probably aren't going to know everything that we want or need from them. Whether it is because we forget to mention something, or because it's something that our unconscious mind has yet to fully reveal, there will always be things to learn about ourselves and our partners.

We might enter a BDSM relationship thinking that we both are only interested in bondage and it turns out that something much more rich, interesting and complex is lurking beneath the surface. It pays to be open and ready to probe that little bit deeper if there are any signs at all that there's an itch that's not being scratched. Be attentive for this.

I guess that being attentive in this way is also a type of service - a service we perform for each other.

Week 15

Growing dependence

Of course it's natural for people to start their BDSM careers with limited skills. But having said that, we should note that newcomers might already have natural ability or flair, or they might have some experience in some other area which they can bring to bear in their BDSM activities such as boating (for knots and bondage), medical training (sounds and catheters), or parenting (bossing people around). But, however knowledgeable or experienced they are when they arrive on BDSM's doorstep, they have to adapt what they know and what they subsequently learn for the completely new reason of establishing a power-, pain- or bondage-based relationship with their partner.

BDSM skills need to be complementary between BDSM partners. For example, a top who throws a whip around is generally going to need someone who can well receive a lashing and not every submissive or bottom can. Likewise, a dominant whose area of interest is a particular type of service is obviously going to need a submissive who can deliver that service and not every submissive is inclined that way. Finally, a master who wishes to train up a slave clearly needs someone who both has the aptitude and the desire to be a slave and who is willing and able to learn.

As well as having these complementary interests, there also needs to be a corresponding level of skill, experience or ability present. A top who is an expert with a whip probably won't find a newbie very satisfying as a partner because the top will have to hold himself back a lot of the time. Similarly, a master who wishes to train a slave won't have a very good time if the slave lacks the discipline to study and practice.

If there isn't this corresponding level of skill, experience or ability between the two people in regards to what they're trying to achieve together, then one person or the other is not going to be able to fully stretch their wings.

Complicating things a little is that over time we learn. Our skills and understanding develop. We have a problem though when one person stops learning or growing and their partner does not.

There can actually be good reasons for someone to not advance or improve. They may not have the time to devote to gaining more skill or understanding or they may simply not have any pressing need to be any better than they are. What they know might be entirely sufficient to satisfy their needs. If they're with a partner who feels the same then more learning or growing might simply be wasted.

For dominants, submissives, masters and slaves a necessary component is an effective partner. A super duper master is not going to be at his super-duperest without a super duper slave. That's not to say that he or she will be a poor master, but they're only going to achieve their fullest when they have a slave who operates at the same or at a higher level.

A consequence of one person stopping or limiting what they learn BDSM-wise is that a partner who needs to go further simply cannot. A master on his way to super-duperdom will slowly grind to a halt if his slave isn't able to grow with him. In a similar way, for a submissive to have a profound experience they generally need confidence that their dominant knows and appreciates what's happening. When they see that their dominant is clearly lagging behind then they're not going to be able to get those profound experiences because it's not safe for them to go there alone just hoping for the best.

There is, I think, an implicit obligation for each of us to grow to prevent these problems. If we don't, or if we assume that what we are is good enough, then we are condemning our partners to stay the same as well. Through learning we open the door to new experiences not only to ourselves, but also to our partners. In BDSM this is vital because so much hangs on the actual interactions we have with others, especially our slaves, submissives, masters and dominants. When we can do more and understand more then we are not only increasing our own horizons, but we are also increasing what our partners can experience with us. We're increasing their horizons as well.

Week 16

Restraining dominance and submission

Physical bondage is awesome.

One of the reasons I say that is because there are so many different ways of doing it.

You can do light bondage, such as by tying your lovely to the bedposts with silk scarves (assuming you are lucky enough to have bedposts). Some people consider blindfolds to be part of bondage and they're just as easy and light to apply at the same time.

You can get a bit more serious and buy yourself some soft cotton rope or cord and start tying ankles together or tying hands behind backs.

You can get more serious still and try out a hogtie.

You can get long pieces of clear kitchen wrap and go for a sort of mummified look with opportune holes in the wrap for easy access to some of the more interesting body parts which may lay inside.

You can use coarse rope, thin rope, thick rope, stretchy rope, string, duct tape (over clothing because duct tape can stick nastily to skin) or even superglue (with a lot of care and please keep some nail polish handy to dissolve it). All these create different sensations.

You can use metal bondage - chains, metal clamps, handcuffs or leg irons. You can even use cages.

You can tie someone loosely so that they can still move around a bit or even so that they can have a chance of escaping... and there are plenty of escapologist submissives bottoms out there, I can assure you.

You can have someone really, really tightly restrained so that can't even wiggle their fingers, or you could put a collar or leg iron on them, attach a long chain between it and a bolt on a wall and then they can move their arms, legs and body around as much as they want - they just can't go very far.

You can do partial restraint. You can tie just one arm. Or you can tie both arms behind their back and leave them to wander the apartment in mild frustration. This can be good at a party where you hang a tray over their neck like the ones cigarette girls used to carry, and have them take around drinks and bring back empty glasses.

You can even have restraint which isn't restraint at all but which feels restraining, such as breast bondage, body harnesses or rope corsets.

Most BDSM and leather folk are familiar with short bondage scenes or even overnight bondage scenes where you keep your tied-up partner in bed with you, but bondage scenes can also be quite long. You can have someone chained up for the whole of a weekend, or longer, and as long as you take care to feed and toilet them it'll be quite fine.

There are many reasons why people do bondage. It can cathartic. It can be empowering. It can create exciting feelings of helplessness. It can be extremely intimate. It can build trust.

One excellent characteristic of bondage is that you can very quickly turn it off. You can undo the ropes, unlock the padlocks or open the cage and the scene is over. This is different to, say, flogging, caning or whipping where bruises, cuts or tenderness can last for days after the last blow.

Oddly though, it's quite common to think of dominance and submission (and mastery and slavery) in quite limited terms even though there's no reason why we can't have a similar variety, similar range and similar breadth of dominance and submission as bondage aficionados have with rope and chains.

Dominance and submission and mastery and slavery aren't limited to single ideas of service, sexual availability, kneeling or special clothing so it's useful to consider and compare the different types of physical bondage which exist to what might be their dominance-and-submission equivalents.

- Micromanaging a slave or a submissive might be like the use of coarse, rough rope in bondage,

- Setting a goal and then letting a slave work out for themselves how they're going to achieve it could be like using soft, cotton rope tied loosely,

- Tying someone, or mummifying them, could be like placing a stationary slave in a corner as decoration or on a table as a candle holder, and

- Switching from formal protocol to casual protocol might be the equivalent of cutting off or loosening part of a rope tie.

What other comparisons can you make?

What we can do is consider that slavery and submission have psychological or spiritual parallels to physical bondage. We can be just as open to finding new ways to explore them as bondage fans are with rope and whatever else they can get their hands on that can be pressed to purpose.

When we do see dominance, submission, mastery or slavery just in terms of service or sex then aren't we actually applying restraints to ourselves in an unproductive way? We're applying a sort of bondage to ourselves which limits what we do but it doesn't lead us to catharsis or empowerment. Instead, it simply keeps us in a little alley while there are streets and even a whole city waiting for us outside.

Week 17

When love gets in the way

There's an interesting challenge for some BDSM enthusiasts: namely having a satisfying or rewarding BDSM relationship with a partner without the complication of love. Or maybe I should say without the complication of being "in love".

The reason why I added that qualification of "in love" is that, a) I think that friends can be eminently well-suited to being BDSM partners, and b) that friends can love each other. I think that there's no reason why a master and a slave can't be really good friends, or why a dominant and a submissive can't be friends either. In fact, building a BDSM relationship on top of a friendship means that you have a head start on trust and respect and this is very good.

But for many people being in love changes things. Maybe it is the case that we humans are predisposed to falling in love with someone we're close to and intimate with, and it's definitely the case that we try to be close to and intimate with our BDSM partners, even if it's not necessarily sexual and even if it does tend to involve pain for some, a lot, or all of the time.

Being "in love" seems to be its own justification and motivation for behaving in certain ways such as wanting to spend a lot of time with someone, looking deeply in their eyes or buying them chocolates. These aren't bad things in themselves and I can certainly see buying chocolates as something a submissive might do anyway, particularly if they're ordered to do so. But being in love really only works when both people are, er, afflicted and want to spend time together, look into each other's eyes and do things for each other. If both aren't in love then for one it becomes problematic and for the other it becomes painful, and not in a good way.

I suppose the nearest parallel we can get to this in vanilla relationships is where a friend falls in love with another friend. While they're friends then they can do things together, even intimate things, and have a great time. But they stay friends and there's a comfortable distance kept between them. There are boundaries which they maintain and they treat each other as separate individuals. It gives them a sort of freedom-through-separation.

When being "in love" enters the picture then it mainly seems to be boundary issues which arise. When someone is in love they don't want the same boundaries which they may have had before as friends. They want more closeness.

Boundaries equals freedom for some people and when someone wants to be too close to them - be it their partner, their friend, their master, their slave, their submissive, or their dominant - then they can find it terribly restrictive.

Falling in love with a BDSM partner can also change the nature of dominance and submission. For example, dominating and torturing may not be quite so appealing any more.

62

I don't think that there's a tablet you can take or an injection you can get which will prevent someone falling in love. It is though something to think about when considering a BDSM relationship. If either you or your partner think being in love is a good idea and the other doesn't then there may be rough seas ahead.

It's something important to discuss with your partner. It may not be something you can predict or forestall, but it can be something you can think about in advance so that if and when it does happen to you or your partner you're not completely surprised and you know how you both feel about it.

Week 18

Who makes the first move?

As a guy in vanilla land many years ago, it used to bug me enormously that the burden fell on me to make the first move to establish a relationship with a girl. This was the role of the guy: To be the one who made the initial overtures. The role of the girls - at least to the best of my knowledge - was to make themselves appealing so that guys would take an interest in them. It was the guys who made the first move and the girls who got to say yea or nay. This was how it was for decades and possibly centuries. It still is to some extent. Why? I don't know, but I'm sure there was a reason.

Anyhow, it occurs to me that a characteristic of the roles in BDSM - such as submissive, dominant, master, slave, top or bottom - is that none of them have this implicit idea that they carry the onus of making the first move and that the others are compelled to wait with hopeful optimism that they are the receivers of such moves.

Maybe it is the case that we BDSM folk have been so preoccupied with developing skills and understandings related to what it is that we do (WIITWD) that no one has formed any preconceptions about who makes the first move. I really like this idea and hope that it is true.

For example, many female submissives are quite happy to reach out to a male dominant who they have never met before either to try to connect or to ask for some "attention". It may well be that a request to have their feet caned, to have infernal objects inserted into dark places or to "try out a violet wand" might be the equivalent of the rather dated, "Would you like to come up and look at my etchings?" but it is still an opening gambit. From this it seems that we BDSM folk are less burdened than our vanilla cousins in regards to gender-based hesitancy to approach one another.

I think it actually is a consequence of involvement in BDSM that this is so for two reasons. Firstly, we are often very aware of what it is that we're looking for. Looks can matter less for us than for vanilla folk. What we are looking for instead is someone who can genuinely engage us rather than someone who would look good hanging on our arm at social events or who would be a good breeder.

Secondly, I think respect has a big part in this. For BDSM activities and relationships to be successful everyone, regardless of at which end of the whip they stand or whether they serve or are served, has to bare their soul to their partner. This means they often expose the parts of themselves which are most sensitive. They need to trust that their partner will respect and value them, and this attitude of respecting a partner is one of the characteristics of what we could call a good member of the BDSM community.

Thus, when someone approaches another BDSM person about engaging in some sort of activity, connection or even relationship, they are more likely to get a careful, considered and respectful response. This, sadly, is not so likely in vanilla land. In vanilla land this lack of respect leads to fear of making the first move.

In regards to the question which is the title of this article: Who makes the first move? I think the answer is that any of us can and should. It isn't the domain of dominants or masters any more than it is the domain of submissives or slaves. In this I think we are all equal and I think it is very important that we should keep it this way.

It's not always obvious what passions, desires or interests await discovery in the person selecting goodies next to us at a snack table at a BDSM party, or in the people we see at workshops or other events. But by respectfully approaching them (emphasis on "respect"), and by being respectful of any who approach us, we can find out without fear. And - who knows? - we may also find a companion, friend or partner to boot.

Week 19

Taking it seriously

I take BDSM very seriously.

It's true that it can be exciting, stimulating, arousing and even a lot of fun. But there can come a time in BDSM play and in BDSM relationships where the stakes rise to a very high level.

For example, if your BDSM play is limited to silk scarves and simple bondage games in bed then you probably don't need to think too much about safety or long-term consequences. On the other hand, if you have progressed to doing heavy impact play such as with canes or whips then you do need to think about safety and long-term consequences. You need to take steps to reduce the risks of infection. You need to make sure you have topical antiseptics to hand during and after play, and you probably need to disinfect the whips and so on after use.

When serious attention to usually-covered body parts is intended then you also need to consider who might see the affected body parts later on: Is a visit to the doctor planned in the next few days and might the doctor see the bruises or weals? Are you planning on going to the beach?

A point I'd like to make here is that this change from light BDSM - such as with silk stockings and fluffy handcuffs - to more intense play can creep up on us. And while our play itself can change, mature and become more intense, sometimes the necessary attitude change in regards to safety and forward planning can lag behind.

I suppose as a parallel you could think about driving: If you're driving a little old car around slow country roads with a friend then the stakes and risks might be low. But when you move to a vehicle with a bit more oomph on the highway then the stakes are not so low any more.

Zooming around on four wheels can be awesome - even more awesome than arriving at your actual, planned destination. The journeys can be profound, funny, intense, satisfying, thought-provoking and life-changing.

But you're in a car and cars are dangerous beasts. If you're not serious about driving then you can have a bad or even deadly accident. The people who are your passengers can pick up on your attitude towards driving and instead of being relaxed and open could be metaphorically clinging to the dashboard with both hands waiting for a slow corner where they can open the door, throw themselves out and leave you hurtling to your doom.

BDSM can be very much like this.

BDSM doesn't just mean physical play such as bondage or wax play or impact play. It also includes psychological play - such as mind fucks - and emotional involvements and relationships. It's just as important to takes these aspects of BDSM seriously as it is the physical aspects.

There are many people, on both sides of the dominant/submissive divide, who have entered the world of BDSM, explored a little,

70

been hurt and then have left, never to return again. It's rarely the physical side of BDSM which causes them to leave. It's usually the psychological or emotional hurt or harm which does it.

The physical side of BDSM is often easy to manage. You can see it, touch it and put a bandage on it. These sorts of risks are things we know well.

The psychological side of BDSM is not so obvious. The injuries and harms which can occur are outcomes which we don't know so well. We might not recognise them, and when we do we might not realise how serious they are. Someone might be left confused, afraid, traumatised or bitter - sometimes without even realising themselves the extent of their own reactions. These are things which are not so straightforward to bandage.

It's easy to progress from the initial stages of BDSM of light bondage, spanking and kinky sex - which don't require much attention - to the more intense, risky and serious activities and relationships without realising that a change of approach is needed to make sure that they're done well, safely and productively for all concerned. This is because there's an often-stealthy evolution of our BDSM play from where it's light and purely physical, to where its effect on us and our partners is emotionally, psychologically and even spiritually profound.

Our planning and consideration of what we do with our BDSM partners shouldn't just be limited to having clean towels and antiseptic to hand. Nor should it be limited to simply knowing how to whack or how to tie and untie knots. Once we move beyond the fluffy handcuff stage of BDSM it's rarely the case that what we do is solely physical. We need to recognise that taking care of each other emotionally and spiritually becomes part of the package as well.

Instead of just looking for marks on the outside we need to also look for them on the inside. And not just with our partners. Questions we should ask include:

- Do I feel happy with what happened? Does my partner?

- Did I get closure? In other words, did everything get said and done which needed to be said and done so that I can move on? Or is there something lingering which needs attending to? Did my partner get closure as well?

- Did things go the way they were planned? Were there any surprises?

The most important thing with BDSM (or anything, really) is that we are happy. Not necessarily that we had a great time or got some excellent jollies, but that we feel happy, really happy.

Anything lingering, or anything that feels not quite right, can mean that things went awry or that doors got opened somewhere in our minds without being properly closed again.

The above questions are worth revisiting on a regular basis for as long as we do BDSM because as what we do evolves, so do the answers, and so does our understanding of what BDSM means to us and how it effects us.

Week 20

Teach your children well

Some years ago I had two friends in the BDSM world who happened to be a married couple. He, J, was the master and she, r, was his slave. I tended to have most to do with r. We often talked about this and that, mutual acquaintances, BDSM principles and so on. It was a good, respectful relationship based on shared interests.

One day I received a message from r saying that a group they were part of had ordered both of them not have anything further to do with me. There was a metaphorical click like a telephone being hung up, and then they were gone.

This order came without warning. The group behind the order never contacted me. I don't know who they were. I don't know why the order was given.

Much time passed and then I unexpectedly received an email from r saying that she and J were moving to England. They were no longer bound by the orders of the group and she wanted to resume contact, catch up and find out how things were going.

In the BDSM and leather worlds the activities and relationships which we share and indulge in often happen behind closed doors, away from scrutiny. They are frequently very private things. In one sense, this is how they should be.

In another sense, this is not how they should be. When I talk of scrutiny, it's not just scrutiny from others to which I refer. What we do, how we live and how we relate to others are things we should scrutinise ourselves. We should look at ourselves and evaluate how well our choices and actions sit with our own personal values. More than that, the choices we make and the actions we do should reflect our own values and be in harmony with them.

This is sometimes easier said than done because there is that terrible evil called temptation which we need to avoid.

Once upon a time I was sitting alone in a gay/lesbian bar just after lunch. I had gone there with a couple of lesbian friends because it was a talent show afternoon and they were going to perform a song. I was sitting on my own while they were backstage preparing and putting on make-up when a woman came over to me and said to me, "My master wants to know if you are gay?" I said no and she walked away.

To me this was odd behaviour for a number of reasons. Firstly, the guy was in the same room as me. How enthusiastic must he be if he can't be bothered getting up to talk to me in person?

Secondly, if he was hoping for some homosexual action involving me, surely it's going to be counterproductive to send a woman over to make the opening move.

Thirdly, and most importantly for the present discussion, it was an inappropriate approach. Maybe in his world every gay and lesbian establishment is a hotbed of leather action with everyone just crying out for a flogging, but this was an otherwise normal bar.

No one was dressed in chaps. No one was decorated with chains. No one was wandering around carrying an armload of floggers or a coil of rope. Everyone was dressed in jeans or similar. In this circumstance is it appropriate to involve a stranger in your own master/slave relationship? I would say it's not.

Would it be appropriate for a slave to ask this same thing - "My master wants to know if you are gay?" - of someone in the local supermarket? After Sunday morning services outside church? At day care? I would suggest it's not appropriate in these places. What then makes it appropriate at a gay/lesbian bar on a pleasant weekend afternoon?

Fourthly, it's just not a winning thing to do. If you were in a vanilla context, in a bar with a couple of friends, would you send one of your friends over to start the process of picking up someone? Would you say, *My first move on that cute chick at the end of the bar would be to sidle up to my friend Joe and ask, "Joe, how about you going over to that lovely lady, pointing me out to her and then asking her if she'd like get to know me?"* Clearly, this is not on. Indeed, were this to go ahead Joe is more likely to be the winner than you.

I actually suspect that this behaviour is a variation of what we see with some parents. They'll drive with their child to the local store, park the car, and then wait in the car and send the kid to do some errand such as to buy something or to return a broken product. Just substitute "slave" for "child" and you have it.

Sending a slave to do errands like these achieves two things for the master. Firstly, it distances them from feedback. If there's a problem with what they've sent the slave to do, the slave has to deal with it. The master avoids any direct involvement or any possible confrontation. Secondly, it saves the master from the physical effort of getting up off his butt.

Unfortunately, it also does a third thing. It sends a subtle message to the slave. It says, *I only have you so that I can send you to do crap errands.* Instead, and perhaps obviously to some, the master should be going and doing these things themselves to serve as an example, to take responsibility, and to encounter, endure and resolve any problems rather than their slave having to do it. It is important especially since their slave isn't really equipped for the errand because: a) they are not the main stakeholder, and b) they can't make all the executive decisions which might need to be made.

Finally, errands like this lead the master towards a pathological and chronic attitude of self-fostered laziness.

What it's actually all about is abusing power for some benefit. John Dalberg-Acton said, "Power tends to corrupt, and absolute power corrupts absolutely." BDSM and leather, mastery and slavery, are often very much about power and that same risk is very much present.

In the case of the master in the gay/lesbian bar, by using his slave as he did it was a cheap way to reach out. It wasn't a good way. It wasn't a way that was likely to have success. But from his side it required very little effort - just a few words to his slave - and there was no other cost to him. There was no risk to him of an unexpected reaction from me because he didn't actually talk to me. There was no consequence for him to do it. It was a throwaway. And it's power used badly on the off chance that I'd be hot for some guy-on-guy action.

This is like the example with which I started this article. I don't know why the group decided to order my friendship with J and r to end. Maybe they had a good reason. Maybe they didn't. Whatever it was, because they didn't communicate with me and because they used their power over J and r to get their way, there was no consequence for them. I didn't get a chance to appeal, object or respond in any way. They isolated themselves from any consequences.

Groups - whether they are formal groups with rules or fees, or whether they're ad hoc groups held together simply by the members having common interests - gain members because the group provides some benefit. It could be that membership of the group gives you access to other people with the same interests as you, or it could be that there's a benefit from numbers such as where membership fees let the group buy something that the individual members couldn't afford individually. For BDSM folk, maybe the group provides connection to other masters and slaves who have similar values, similar experience or training, or similar awareness. Whatever it is, this provides a motivation for members to follow the directions of the higher-ups in the group, even if you don't agree with them, because if you don't toe the line you risk losing the benefits.

I don't know why J and r followed the directions of the group to break contact with me. Maybe they'd given their word to follow the dictates of the group when they joined and because they were honourable folk that's what they did. Or maybe the benefits of being in the group, possibly other important friendships, were at risk if they didn't follow the order. I'm confident that they didn't want to break contact with me because as soon as the group was out of the picture they got back in contact. Unfortunately, J and r left the country soon after they were liberated from this controlling group and I didn't have a chance to revisit the past with them and find out if they knew why they had been given the order they had.

More than likely, I think, this order was an abuse of power by the group. After all, you probably wouldn't join a group expecting that they'd decide who your friends were once you were a member so an order doing precisely that would seem inappropriate.

I think there are a few reasons why these sorts of situations arise.

One is that we BDSM folk aren't surrounded by examples of better ways of doing things. In vanilla land we see lots of other people around us having relationships, interacting with each other, and we see examples of what works and what doesn't. We frequently see what happens when things aren't done well. In media and on television we have shows where moral messages are part of the entertainment. We BDSM folk don't have that. We don't have TV shows with profound scenes like this:

> Young master: I'm not happy with all the time my slave is spending with her friend Jamie so I'm going to order her to end the relationship.
>
> Wise master: That's not such a good idea. Have you really thought about this?
>
> Young master: Sure I have. She's my slave. I can do what I want with her.
>
> Wise master: That may be true, but have you checked with Jamie to see how she would feel about this?
>
> Young master: No. Why should I? She's not my slave. I don't even know her.
>
> Wise master: That's exactly the point. Just having a slave and bossing them around doesn't make you a master. Being in charge and taking responsibility for the consequences of your actions is being a master. And if you don't know Jamie, then you don't know what sort of consequences there are going to be when you cut off her relationship with your slave.

Young master: I don't have time to do that.

Wise master: Then you don't have time to really be a master.

It would be nice if there was a BDSM or leather channel on cable TV which had shows like "Life With Master" or "The Slave Show" where issues could be aired and shared. But we don't have that. What we often have instead is people getting into BDSM on their own and then having to make up their own rules of behaviour and values because there are few-to-no examples available for them to learn from. Even with the best intentions they can't appreciate every aspect of BDSM. Often in ignorance they decide something is a good idea and don't have any way of learning that it isn't.

This reminds me of a story I tell from time to time about a master at a BDSM conference I once attended. He did a presentation on fire play and demonstrated it with a well-endowed young lady sitting topless in a straight-backed chair. He smeared some flammable fluid on her boobs and lit it. A couple of other masters in the front row quickly put a stop to the demonstration because: a) there was a serious risk of the girl inhaling the flames rising up towards her face, and b) because there was a serious risk of setting her long hair on fire. The master doing the demo hadn't known about these risks. He hadn't thought about them. He'd developed his understanding of fire play simply by doing it. In the little town where he lived there wasn't anyone more experienced to enlighten him and it was only luck which had prevented him having an accident before this.

Without the benefit of accumulated experience, it's a hard or even impossible ask to invent or discover what's right and create your own rules.

It doesn't have to be this way, at least not as much as it is.

At times and for various reasons, such as the law or social acceptance, we do need to hide our BDSM relationships and activities from some people. But not all people. Even for folk who only have a very private BDSM relationship with one partner, it's important to have opportunities to share and learn from others. Who knows, maybe dangling your male slave upside down by his testicles for a couple of hours isn't such a good idea after all and you've been lucky so far.

If any of your master/slave activities involve anyone else in any way - if you give orders which might affect them - make sure they know what's going on and that you get feedback so you know things are working (or not).

By making sure we talk... and listen, we increase the chances we get things right, even without always realising it. In a way we BDSM folk are disadvantaged because isolation is common for us. Because of this we need to make the extra effort to ensure that we are doing the right things by design and not by accident, and that our choices are really socially responsible in a wide sense and not just things which seem OK at the time.

A number of people who have read my work have observed that I seem like an introvert. This is, in fact, quite true. And like many introverts I only have a very small number of friends. They are very important to me. One of my two closest friends is A, now an ex-slave.

Many years ago, A was ordered by her then-master to end our friendship. Again, this was a situation where I didn't know the guy. I got the message, no explanation of why, and then she was gone. It was actually quite devastating and distressing for me because we were very close and spoke frequently. For me it was very much like she had suddenly died and it took me quite a while to get over this.

Six months later he changed his mind and she was back. I never found out why he had this change of heart. However, I can say that my friendship with A lasted many years beyond the end of his mastery of her.

It is perhaps telling that while I actually know an awful lot of masters and slaves, the only people who behave like this are people whose faces I have never seen.

It is very easy to operate in the dark, in secret in BDSM. But by doing so it creates a fertile ground for inappropriate behaviours and attitudes to develop because there is no oversight. Stepping out from the dark into the light forces oversight, reflection and criticism.

There used to be a local submissive cabal here in Australia. I suspect that there were others elsewhere, but I mention this particular one because I was personally affected by it. This cabal was a group of disaffected female submissives who would get together, either in person or online, and bad-mouth and lie about dominants and masters who didn't do what they wanted. This could be because the dominant didn't "play" with them, or because he had broken up with someone they knew, and so on. It was basically a group of submissives who self-authorised themselves to abuse dominants. This extended to actual property damage.

They would also operate in the dark, either anonymously online or they would talk about the dominants behind their backs or in fora which the dominants didn't frequent. I had reports from submissive friends of mine about their activities and they weren't nice. As well as focussing on me and other local dominants and masters, a very respectable master I knew ended up in court after property of his (his car) was damaged one night.

Their intention was to be deliberately malicious. Fortunately they're gone now.

But even being part of a well-intentioned group doesn't automatically prevent bad behaviours. The master I mentioned above, the then-master of A, was part of what was, as far as I could tell, a loose collection of individuals, leather families and houses. At the time they had a rather grandiose name for themselves. I don't know if they still exist, but back then it was claimed they had over a thousand members around the world. I used to think that having this many people united would create a sort of continuity which the smaller and isolated pockets of BDSM enthusiasts seem to lack. It could be one in which understanding could develop and be handed down, where sharing would create a better understanding of what is right. But alas, no.

It turned out that they were rather secretive and closed and this was not conducive to right behaviour, regardless of intention.

Recently, I was watching a talk by an Arab-American comedienne who has cerebral palsy[1]. She commented that as she was growing up no one made fun of her disability. It's only when she became known that she started to receive insults from the Internet. The Internet can be a dark place and people can say things with effective anonymity… and they did. She made an interesting and very relevant point saying that, "maybe it still takes a village to teach our children well".

What we have in our nowadays BDSM world is individuals and small groups frequently disconnected from each other. We need to find a way to include them so that we become a large village community, where we can know each other, share by example and

---

[1]Maysoon Zayid: I got 99 problems… palsy is just one
http://www.ted.com/talks/…
maysoon_zayid_i_got_99_problems_palsy_is_just_one.html

learn what is right or wrong for us all. Just doing stuff in isolated pockets doesn't work.

It's interesting that workshops and demonstrations are common events in BDSM but courses on honour, respect and trust are not popular in the BDSM or leather worlds. Bondage and flogging - they're popular, but honour, respect and trust seem to be things best taught by example and to do this we need to get together.

I don't know that there's a solution we can simply apply which will make all the problems I mentioned go away. What we can do though, are a number of things which will help:

1. Don't operate in the dark. Make an effort not to hide what you're doing, and make sure that you are on the front line when there are consequences to what you do,

2. Try to provide a good example to others,

3. Discuss situations and problems with others, especially others outside of your group. People in your group are likely to be supportive of you regardless both because you're in their group, and because they're likely to have similar opinions to yours. This is not always what is most helpful. You are going to learn more from people who have different opinions to your own, not from people who agree with you,

4. When what you do involves anyone else - in any way at all - reflect on the impact on them: friends and relatives of slaves, people who live nearby, friends and relatives of masters, and so on. Think as widely afield as possible. If in doubt, ask. Even if you're sure, ask anyway,

5. Share your understandings with others. Especially be prepared to put what you do and your attitudes under the microscope for others to examine and criticise,

6. Consider how to work with others to develop and share values and understanding over the long term.

It's very easy to think of plausible-sounding reasons not to do the right thing. If any of you reading this have something you know you should do but don't want to do, contact me and I'll quickly come up with plausible-sounding reasons to help you avoid whatever it is: Maybe you're not feeling well, maybe you have an important meeting coming up elsewhere and you need to be rested and have a clear head for it, maybe we can say someone else should be doing it instead of you, maybe we can say that it's not appropriate for you to get involved, maybe it's now too late for it to be done and it was someone else's fault for not asking sooner. See how easy it is to come up with excuses?

The issue is not the dexterity with which someone comes up with reasons to avoid doing the right thing. What is important is how hard they'll work to make sure that they don't avoid it. Make no mistake, doing the right thing often involves actual work. It can be hard, and it can frequently involve you being brutally honest with yourself. Yes, it's often easier not to do the right thing, but it's not right.

And remember, being able to do something doesn't mean that you should.

This is especially important in BDSM where we can easily arrange for things to be done out of sight so that we're not subject to scrutiny. The master who sent his slave to check if I was gay, the people who ordered my master and slave friends to not contact me, and the master who ordered my close friend to end our friendship are all examples of this. I'm sure, if you asked any of them, that they'd have excellent-sounding reasons for doing what they did. That's not the point.

Stepping out from the dark into the light compels oversight, reflection and criticism. These are good things. We need these. We need our village to be illuminated by ideas, shared experiences and open discussion. We need to get rid of the dark areas, the hidden spaces. We need to make a special effort to open them up and keep them open.

So. What are things like in your village?

Week 21

Listen to yourself

It's really only a teeny-tiny fraction of what we do which has to do with our rational or intellectual selves. Most of the time these aren't the areas which we're aiming at when we're looking for stimulation, arousal or satisfaction. We don't look at our BDSM activities as involving intricate or complex puzzles to solve, or as exercises requiring obscure knowledge of history, science or mathematics. It's why I wrote in one of my books that you don't find Scrabble^{TM} sets or chess boards in dungeons or at BDSM play parties. Much of what we do isn't aimed at our rational, intellectual or even necessarily sensible selves. It's aimed at our primal drives, our gut, our lizard brains, our unconscious minds.

It's the rational and intellectual parts of our brains which are generally in charge in the words department. They're the bits which put together and say sentences, and they're the bits which listen to the sentences other people say to us and make sense of them. Our primal sides, our guts and our lizard brains generally only rise to a level of communication involving "Ugh!", "Mmmmm", smiles, frowns and physical action. Well... it's actually a lot richer communication than that, but my point is that it generally doesn't involve great verbal eloquence. Shakespeare didn't delve into trying to express primal drives in words. We don't read in any of his works, "Forsooth! What beckons on the horizon? 'Tis an orgasm!" No. Words don't work in this particular realm.

This makes understanding our partners' needs challenging at times. When words can't always express what we want, need or feel, how can we get the message across to them? People who do stuff in dungeons often either use pre-agreed signals or just plain familiarity with their partner to guide what they do. They know that trying to use words, trying to explain something in the heat or passion of the moment can be an excellent way to kill the mood.

Is there another way?

Yes, there is.

A thing we should recognise is that in these times when primal drives are being expressed, when deeper urges are holding sway, when our rational mind has moved to the back-burner and our gut is in charge we don't grunt, groan, wince, cringe, tense up, growl, touch, reach out or make any of these other nonverbal expressions just because they're a way of letting off steam. They're actually our gut and our lizard brain trying to communicate.

Our rational mind and our intellect communicate with well-chosen words, but our unconscious mind uses actions, facial expressions, vocalisations and gestures. And just as our rational mind targets our partner's rational mind with words, our unconscious mind and our primal drives yell out to our partner's unconscious mind and primal side not with words, but with actions, facial expressions, vocalisations, and so on.

Our unconscious minds use nonverbal language to communicate with the unconscious of our partners. You could, I suppose, take the time to study your partner, make a note of all the nonverbal expressions they use, put them in a chart and then work out what each one means: "long, low moan = need more bamboo under fingernails; shaking uncontrollable = either cold, having orgasm, or having fit; completely limp: possibly dead, hide body."

The problems with doing this are that it takes a lot of time and you can easily get it wrong, you have to create a new chart for every partner, and it's distracting for you because while they're in the throes of passion or excitement when you should ideally be involved, you're instead wearing your white coat, acting like a lab technician and analysing everything they do.

This chart and analytical business is actually you trying to use your intellect to make sense of primal drives and gut. Why do this when you have a built-in receiver that understands your partner's primal language already?

I'm talking about your own primal side, your own gut and your own unconscious. Your partner doesn't wave their arms around and make funny noises just to pass the time. They're trying to send you a message, and often without even realising it you receive that message from them. They're talking in primal-speak, and your unconscious mind can hear and understand it.

All you have to do is make sure that you listen and don't get in the way.

When you are with your partner - doing something diabolical, no doubt - and you suddenly feel an urge to grab them, handle them roughly or throw them against the wall; or you suddenly feel an overwhelming urge to have your wicked sexual way with them, these feelings are probably not all your own work. Your partner probably did something, made a sound, showed some facial expression or moved in some particular way that helped trigger you. Part of your mind "heard" them and reacted.

This is a good thing. It means that you are in tune with your partner. Assuming they weren't shocked about what you did, or they didn't suddenly get mightily pissed off with what you did, it meant that you got it right.

By quietening your own mind and by learning to notice changes in yourself you can recognise when your partner is sending out primal or unconscious signals. These may not always rise to an intense call-to-arms as can happen during play time, but by recognising your own responses - even when you're in some non-BDSM environment like a supermarket - you can say to yourself, "Hmmm. Snookums is apparently in the mood for XYZ." This awareness lets you act in a positive and productive way, even if it's just to acknowledge that you got the message with a simple stroke of their neck or a brief lowering of yourself such as by bending down in front of them to adjust your shoes. You might also make a note to yourself to do something about it when you both get home.

This is about listening to yourself. When your partner starts sending, your own primal receiver will react. Listen to it, to your feelings and to your gut. When these change and your partner is nearby or talking to you, there's a good chance that there's something other than words going on and you're reacting to that. Listen closely to what's inside you. It's your biggest clue to what your partner is feeling and to what they need.

Week 22

Disempowering through invention

It may not come as a shock to you to when I say that I have a keen interest in mastery.

In particular, there are two aspects of mastery that I focus on. They are:

1. Understanding it, and

2. Increasing it.

There's a very insidious phrase which is the nemesis of these two goals. It easily slips into conversations and it can sound surprisingly innocent. It's usually uttered in response to "why" questions such as, "Why does ABC happen?" or "Why do some submissives do XYZ?" This evil phrase goes something like this:

"Because that's the way it is."

This answer is an invention. It's simply made up by the person who said it. It's not a real answer to the question. In reality it's actually a poor alternative to saying, "I don't know."

The nasty thing about this evil phrase is that it creates a block to moving forwards towards understanding. And in doing so it also creates a block to moving forward towards mastery.

Let me clarify this a little.

When someone says, "Because that's the way it is," what they're asserting is that the answer to a question is unknowable. In many cases they're making this claim so that everyone who hears them thinks that this is actually the case.

By doing this they create an oddly level playing field for themselves. If a master can convince others that something is unknowable he removes a threat to himself. This threat is that someone else will gain superior knowledge. If someone else gains superior knowledge then this master is knocked a rung or two down from the position he's trying to maintain. By encouraging ignorance in others he makes sure that no one rises above him.

Let me give you an example. Let's take the question: "Why do some submissives respond well to being caned on their rear end and others not?" Now let's imagine a group of BDSM folk including one Master Hercules (a name he chose because he sees himself as mighty). If Master Hercules doesn't know the answer to this question (and it's clearly a good question for a master to know the answer to) and somebody asks it, then it's very much in Master Hercules' interest to say, "Because that's the way it is." The reason is that if others in the group, particularly his own submissive(s), consider the question and come up with an answer, then Master Hercules immediately doesn't look so mighty any more.

Now Master Hercules might have actually considered this question already and not found an answer. He may have even convinced himself that there isn't an answer, hence his reply.

Making this "it's unknowable" claim also disempowers the master or dominant. When Master Hercules says that XYZ is unknowable, then Master Hercules can never be a master of XYZ. He has created a belief in his own mind that prevents him from becoming a master of XYZ. If, instead, Master Hercules were to say that he doesn't know XYZ, then the possibility of becoming a master of XYZ remains attainable and on his horizon. He may not master it today. He may not master it tomorrow. But it's there. When he instead says that XYZ is unknowable then he has completely removed it from his horizon and he cannot strive to attain it. And this defeat of himself is something which he has done to himself. On his own. No one helped. He defeated himself.

In my own journey I discovered that increasing mastery is not so much about actually making it grow, but is more about getting rid of the things which prevent it growing in the first place. This amounts to the avoidance or dismantling of contexts which inhibit mastery, and by actively creating or engaging in contexts which cause it to flourish.

One of the points I made in another essay[1] is that a master or dominant creates a context in which their slave can come out and blossom. While it's true that our submissives and slaves are in a position to help create contexts where we can really shine (or flourish) as dominants and masters, the opportunities for self-sabotage are firmly in our own hands. Saying, "Because that's the way it is," is one of these self-sabotage techniques.

---

[1]Enslavement on page 9.

One of things I try to do with "why" questions I can't answer is say this: "I don't know the answer today. Maybe I won't know it tomorrow either, but someday I will."

In fact, I like to have questions to which I don't know the answer today. I like to listen to others because when I hear, "Because that's the way it is," I know that I have just encountered something, possibly golden, which I definitely need to explore.

There are variations of this evil phrase. Here are some of the variations I listen out for:

- "I don't think there really is an answer to this",

- "Ultimately your main question is not one that can be answered. Try to explain why some people don't like chocolate",

- "Because I'm wired that way",

- "The answer simply is that it's how their brain works", and

- "But at some point you simply accept some people like things others do not".

Keep in mind that the people who say these things might genuinely believe that they are enlightening you by telling you you are not going to find an answer. Often though, what they're doing is discouraging you from looking further.

Week 23

Overanalysing? There ain't no such thing!

Some people read my writing and criticise saying that I overanalyse. They say that living in the moment is the right way to go.

For me it's like looking at a beautiful painting.

If you see it in a gallery, you look at it and the beauty washes over you and you can submerge yourself in that moment. This is awesome.

If you see it in a gallery and a guide explains the history of the artist and some of the features of the painting then the beauty still washes over you plus you come to appreciate the circumstances around the painting's existence and you value it even more.

If you see it in a gallery and you have an education in art, then when you see the painting its beauty washes over you like before, plus you look at it and see it not as a sole item but as part of a continuum of art history and as part of the evolution of the artist himself (or herself, of course). You also look at the detail of the execution, how it has been painted, the choice of colours, the mood the artist has managed to instill in the painting and you get even more out of it.

When you see a painting and you don't know these things you are compelled to see it only one way.

When you do have that education, that knowledge, that training, that experience, that awareness then you can still see the beauty, plus you have the choice of seeing a whole lot more.

I think this adds to the moment rather than takes away from it.

While I don't advocate that everyone study art history or that everyone explores principles, psychology and philosophy of BDSM to the extent I do, I think we need to recognise that there is a continuum of understanding. Some people are happy just with the immediate experience of BDSM, with doing a scene and then moving on to the next one. The depth in their life may lie somewhere else and so flitting from scene to scene, so to speak, is perfectly fine for them. For others, their life's journey may involve them immersing themselves completely. Learning, analysing, and even what others might call overanalysing is part of their own growth and it lets them squeeze the most out of their BDSM.

I think that anyone who is anywhere on this continuum has a place in BDSM. Regardless of where you lie on this continuum - at one end, the other, or somewhere in the middle - you are just as much a part of BDSM as anyone else.

Week 24

I like assertive submissives

I don't feel threatened by assertive submissives or slaves. On the contrary, I quite like them.

I think that it makes them more interesting and more demanding in a good way. I like them to be intelligent, to have a mind of their own, and I like them to have good-to-high standards.

For me BDSM - and much of life in general - is an opportunity to challenge myself and to grow. But when I say challenge, I don't mean challenge as in challenging my authority, being a tease, or being a smart-ass. It's about helping me have opportunities to improve myself so that I can then take better advantage of what the world has to offer.

I don't consider submissives as being there solely as targets for my mighty and masterly will. Of course, they are such targets *sometimes* and I think it's important to regularly exercise my mighty and mastery will so that it stays the fresh, invigorated and finely-honed implement that it is and doesn't become listless or flabby.

But a submissive or slave being thoughtful, intelligent and opinionated is actually what I call a service. A cluey and experienced slave can keep me on my toes and draw my attention to things that I may have slipped up on. It's not just their body that's at my service, nor is it just their ability to carry heavy packages or run errands, and nor is it just their ability to tirelessly suck cock like an industrial vacuum cleaner. I look for and expect an intelligent and incisive mind to be there at my beck and call as well.

And having that intelligent and incisive mind available, I don't put it to use with make-work like solving algebra problems or hunting for new prime numbers. Much more useful to me is having that mind active and involved with what I'm doing, part of my projects with me, equally knocking crap ideas on the head as much as she supports and helps me develop good ones. It's important that at all times she's aware of this, just as much as she's aware of who wears the pants (so to speak):

> Her: "Master, I don't think this is right."
>
> Me: "Thank you for letting me know, however keep licking and I'll fix it up later."

I don't think that there's a conflict between being submissive or slave and being assertive. In fact, I don't think that there's any connection between assertiveness and submissiveness or between assertiveness and slaviness.

My dictionary says that "assertiveness" is about "having or showing a confident and forceful personality". There's no problem there as far as I'm concerned. No one ever told me that being a master was going to be easy and having a strong and confident partner is a good thing in my books. I don't want a doormat.

I mean, I know plenty of doormats. Some of them are quite interesting, intelligent and attractive people. And there's a place for them in BDSM, which I suppose you could say is underfoot. But the service I'm interested in personally is being challenging.

Shy and timid can be appealing, especially in young submissives, but only for a short time. Overall, I prefer submissives who are confident, assertive and who are keen to make themselves part of my team, even if it is just the two of us. It can be difficult, if not impossible, to form a team otherwise.

Week 25

How much?

How much BDSM is enough BDSM?

Some things don't have a BDSM component. The garbage may need to be taken out, hair might need to be washed, shopping may need to be done, or the car may need to be filled with petrol. These things are very difficult to do submissively or dominantly. They're things you just do.

On the other hand, things like bondage, cages, flogging, formal protocol and service are chock full of BDSM.

It means that through the course of the day we can have opportunities which are very BDSM-ey (pronounced "B-D-S-M-ee") interspersed with things which aren't BDSM-ey at all.

How do we find a balance?

It becomes a bit more complicated when we consider that not all BDSM is the same. Wielding a mighty flogger against a submissive's bare and receptive posterior is not like tying them up and dangling them from the ceiling, the same as eating lasagne isn't like eating grilled fish. Well, that's a sort of pointless food comparison there, but what I'm trying to say is that some people don't like lasagne anyway and may want to do piercing or an intense sexual deprivation scene instead.

Is it appropriate then to have a sort of BDSM diet planned ahead of time, maybe a weekly or monthly calendar showing the BDSM delights we're planning on consuming? Every second Monday we might dangle heavy weights off a pair of convenient labia. On Thursdays we do an hour of metal bondage followed by some testicle fondling. Most evenings it's then dinner served in a french maid's outfit and on Fridays it's the dominant who wears the outfit. Weekday mornings we start the day with some grovelling and on Saturdays and Sundays a little bit of golden showers in the bathroom.

Is that too organised? Should it be more spontaneous? Should we maybe do it like take-away with a menu stuck to the fridge door and each evening we go up to the menu and say, "Hmmmm. Tonight I think I'll have a serving of intense impact play with a side order of boob torture. And then I think I'd like to finish off with some quick fornication."

It's clear that when you're in the dungeon or tangled up in rope, or when you're knee-deep in evil torture devices and vibrators in the bedroom that you want your BDSM to be on, On, ON!

Do you want it on all the time? Should it ever be completely off, or can it simply be on the back burner or hidden away? I know dominant/submissive couples who, when visiting their vanilla families, still stay as dominant and submissive, but just play it out in a more socially acceptable way by deferring respectively (submissive) or asking politely (dominant).

I think that a combination of spontaneous and planned BDSM is the best. Allowing yourselves to be spontaneous allows you to take adantage of unexpected urges and unplanned opportunities, while planned activities allow you to savour the build-up to and expectation of what is to come.

Above all though, I think the most important thing is to make sure that there's always quality time and energy so that your BDSM wants and needs can get met fully without it seeming like you fit it in between other engagements. In other words, make sure that you give your BDSM the priority it deserves.

Week 26

Bedroom-only BDSM

As we all know, "BDSM" is actually an acronym. It stands for "Bedroom and Dungeon Sex and Masturbation". Or, at least, that's what it seems to be for many people. If you look through the profiles of BDSM people online, many of them seem to be looking for BDSM only in the bedroom... hence the "B".

It's true that there can be an intensity when you combine sexual drives with BDSM which can be hard to get outside of the bedroom or dungeon, but that doesn't mean that BDSM necessarily ends where the rest of the house or apartment begins.

But by leaving the actual nookie, sex, fucking and masturbation behind when you leave the dungeon you're better able to experience and immerse yourself in other aspects of BDSM, aspects which are often drowned out - so to speak - by the intensity of sex.

These are aspects like personal service or surrender. Indeed, personal service - serving your partner or being served by them - can be much more wide-ranging than sex. By putting aside the sex part, at least temporarily, you can explore more subtle types of service, such as personal assistance, working on projects, teaching or training, errands, cooking, anticipating and meeting your partner's wants and needs before they're aware of them themselves, and much more. These are all areas which can be very satisfying and rewarding for someone who is service oriented, but they're hard to focus on and do well when you're naked and on the edge of orgasmic hysteria.

Some people feel obligated to have sex as part of BDSM. This can be because they or their partner genuinely believe that sex and BDSM must go together and they can't conceive of anything else.

Other people keep BDSM and sex together because it means that when they leave the dungeon or bedroom they can leave their BDSM there. It makes life simpler. They don't have to be concerned about any of the complications (they think) of having a dominant/submissive or master/slave relationship. This can be quite valid if they and their partner either don't live together or don't actually have the time or energy to devote to a fully-blown BDSM relationship. Limiting their BDSM to the bedroom and to scenes makes it all much more manageable.

More than this, limiting BDSM to the bedroom is a safety mechanism for some people. Having the possibility of that same intensity outside of the bedroom as inside can be scary. It threatens the routines and rhythms of life and risks displacing them with something new and unknown. Who knows? They may actually like it and maybe that's frightening to consider.

So, do you limit your BDSM activities and relationships to the bedroom or dungeon? Is the rest of your life a BDSM-free zone? Or are you someone who lives their BDSM wherever you happen to be?

Week 27

Paying attention

Attention is a limited resource. When we pay attention to one thing we can't be paying attention to other things. This doesn't mean that we can't multitask. We can, of course, otherwise it'd be challenging to walk and talk at the same time. Although we might not realise it, we see this one-track attention issue all the time such as when we are walking and talking and come to a corner and need to decide which way to go. We say to the person we're with, "Hold on a moment while I work out which way to go," and then we go silent - i.e., we stop talking so we can focus our attention, even if just briefly, onto the problem of where we're going. Then, once we've looked at all the street signs and thought a bit, we make the hopefully-correct turn and then we can start talking again until our attention needs to be used for something else.

The fact that we do this is relevant to our BDSM lives and activities in a number of ways.

If we're delightfully occupied in our dungeon with a partner and we have problems or concerns which we can't manage to leave outside - such as financial woes, family problems or health concerns - then we can't give our full attention to the activities at hand. This is because part of our available attention is being spent on things outside of the dungeon and as a result the actual amount of delight we and our partner can get inside of the dungeon suffers.

I would guess that most of us are aware of this particular problem and we know that there really is only one solution, namely not going into the dungeon until the problems are sorted and we can focus our full attention where it needs to be.

Secondly, because attention is limited it's good to plan ahead. If we stay with the dungeon as an example then we can say that if we have something challenging or complex in mind we're going to be able to devote more of our attention inside the dungeon if we've organised as much as possible ahead of time. For dominants, this might mean planning out a sequence if activities and laying out the appropriate array of diabolical implements so they're ready to grab when we need them. For submissives, this can mean planning ahead of time how we're going to manage pain or prolong our endurance.

Going back to the walking-and-talking example above, if we've planned the route before we started the walk then we don't have to stop our conversation at corners. We already know which way to turn. It's the same in a dungeon: If we've already got everything to hand then we don't have to stop the BDSM "conversation" we're having with our submissive or dominant. It just keeps on going, full steam ahead, without distractions.

It's not necessary to do this planning ahead all the time. Indeed, I think that ad hoc and spontaneous activities can be quite exciting and definitely shouldn't be neglected. But for something complex or for something which we want to last for many hours or even days, then planning ahead means we can focus our attention more on the pleasurable and exciting aspects during the scenes and less on management.

Thirdly, an important thing to say is that there's a difference between toiling and achieving. When we have a difficult problem, particularly a relationship problem, it can be easy to focus our attention on the wrong things. It's easy to focus on the wrong things because it allows you to say to yourself that you're working hard on the problem. While sweat may be pouring from your brow, you don't actually move forward because what you've chosen to do doesn't have any chance of changing or fixing things.

A classic example of this is where a couple into bondage or pain play starts to have relationship problems. These problems may be that one or both of them starts to feel restless or dissatisfied. To deal with this they start doing more bondage or pain play scenes, and more scenes, and ever more scenes. They focus their attention on these scenes because they know how to do them. They're things they're familiar with, things that are comfortable to do even though they're hard to do and even if these activities require a lot of sweat and toil to do. And in spite of a lot of effort going into these activities they may not be the right things to do to solve whatever problem the couple has. Most likely, more of what they're already doing isn't going to be the answer.

So, if paying more attention to something that you're already paying a lot of attention to isn't making things better, step back and find something else to focus on which will.

Like so many things, attention - being able to attend to things - is something we have and which we can use to make our BDSM and our relationships better. But we only have so much. Are you spending your attention wisely?

Week 28

Kinky sex

It seems to me that kinky sex is simply an active search for sexual expression and experience through non-conventional means.

This definition means that what kinky sex is actually depends on the person you're talking to and what they think is conventional. Some very conservative people might think that doggy-style sex is kinky while more liberal-minded folk might only start thinking "kinky" when it involves dressing like a clown.

And I suppose that there'd be some folk who'd think that sex between a man and a woman, where they're both on a bed, where the guy's on top, she's on her back and they're face to face, is kinky sex.

But for some of us BDSM folk, sex has another obvious role beyond both making our nether regions feel extraordinarily good and making new BDSM enthusiasts. It's the power which sex has which we can use as a tool in our explorations of authority.

I would take a wild guess and say that sex is so powerful for us humans because Mother Nature, God or whichever kinky deity you subscribe to wanted the human race to go forth and multiply and what better way to ensure that happens than by making multiplication an exceptionally pleasurable and intense form of arithmetic?

So, because we have this drive to get down and boogie, manipulating opportunities to do "it" and controlling how "it" is done are both excellent ways to drive home - so to speak - the authority, power and control we BDSM folk strive to experience.

I think though, that it's worth comparing these two goals of sex and see how they fit in with what it is that each of us does in our BDSM lives and play.

On the one hand we use sexual activities to satisfy sexual needs. On the other hand, we use sexual activities to either assert authority or control over our partner or to subject ourselves to our partner's authority or control. In some cases, probably a lot of them, we do both at the same time.

It is easy for these two very different goals to blur. It can be that we start seeing BDSM just as a superior way of scratching the itch our pink bits feel. And, of course, combining rope play, a flogger and some lubrication can very easily lead to more intense sex than the horizontal hula just on its own. But we're not just after super sex. We're also exploring domination, mastery, surrender and submission. Or, at least, we should be if we're calling ourselves BDSMers.

Sex is awesome, and I'd never say anything to diminish its value. But it is important to not allow what we could call straight sexual satisfaction and the hunt for the mighty orgasm to get in the way of that other experience we BDSM folk pursue, namely the above mentioned explorations and feelings of mastery, slavery, dominance and submission. These can be equally or even more important for some folk, but the intensity of sexual feelings can be an exciting and seductive lure away from them.

So, with this introduction, I'd like to pose some questions for you to think about in regards to sex - straight and kinky - in your own BDSM life and relationships:

- Is it possible to have vanilla sex in your BDSM relationship?

- Does sex need to be a part of BDSM? It's true that sex can be both an intense experience and a powerful tool in a BDSM context, but is it a requirement?

- What purpose does sex serve in your BDSM relationship? Does it have to do with service? Does it have to do with authority or power? Does it have to do with surrender?

- What is the experience of sex for a dominant, and how does this compare to sex for a submissive? Does gender affect this?

I think we should think about such questions from time to time to help us remember that we're often using sex to satisfy very different needs. We should be careful that we don't let any of them become neglected.

Week 29

(Ab)using ignorance

I've seen some dominants who keep their submissive in the dark as a way to stay in control. Keeping a submissive in the dark, keeping secrets or trying to be mysterious are all ways to disempower a submissive. It might mean that the dominant is in a stronger position relatively, but they've only got there by putting their submissive in a weaker one.

It can be very, very tempting for a dominant to behave this way because one of the questions which regularly faces many dominants is how much do they tell their submissive? In the grand scheme of things it can seem that the dominant must be super confident, have all their moves planned in advance, be extremely knowledgeable or even omniscient, be as empathic as Counselor Troi[1] and be as wise as Buddha's personal guru.

Truth be told, there aren't many dominants like this.

---

[1] A reference to Star Trek: The Next Generation... which is a TV series from the 90's for you who don't know it.

There are however, many dominants who think that as far as their submissive is concerned they shouldn't make mistakes, shouldn't second guess themselves and should always have the answer. Any less feels like it is a sign of weakness and if their submissive noticed this then the dominant's authority would crumble, the relationship would suffer, there would be earthquakes and tidal waves and the end of the world would ensue.

These dominants may see only two solutions to this problem:

1. Become perfect, or

2. Appear to be perfect by hiding their imperfections.

It's not a bad thing to be imperfect, to make mistakes or have more to learn. Admitting that you have made a mistake or don't know something is the first step to overcoming it.

It is definitely not a first step if you don't admit your mistake or ignorance and instead try to hide it from your submissive or use some sleight of hand so that they don't see it. Your submissive is your partner. There's probably a very good chance that this partner is intelligent, smart and has some experience of their own in dealing with mistakes and imperfections. They may even know the solution to any situation you manage to get yourself into.

If you don't keep them in the loop then instead of this partnership having two people working on making it a success there's only one: you. You have reduced the potential effectiveness of this partnership by 50% by excluding your partner.

Your submissive is not expecting you to be perfect or to know all the answers. They're there to help and support you, even when you mess up.

More than that, they're not dumb. There's a very good chance they're going to realise what's happening even if you don't tell them. Trying to hide it won't make you appear to be Super Dom but instead will make you look a bit of a dick (even if you're a woman).

Ignorance is never a good tool for a dominant to have in his toybag. Sweeping mistakes or lack of knowledge under the rug isn't a good way to take charge and that is, after all, what we dominants do.

While I don't advocate reeling off great lists of your foibles to your submissive every chance you get, I do suggest not going out of your way to hide them. If the context comes up when it's right to mention things, or when you think it's useful to explain to your submissive what you're doing, don't leave out your own shortcomings if they're a valid part of the story.

Remember: Your submissive is going to be most effective for you when you empower them. Ignorance is not empowerment and deliberately using ignorance is not control.

Week 30

Caring about BDSM

There are some people, including myself, who call BDSM a lifestyle. It's something which we can integrate into most aspects of our lives and relationships. For other people this side of BDSM is not obvious. For these other people this side of BDSM may not even be believable because they can see BDSM only in terms of shiny black clothing, exotic furniture, predispositions towards rope or unusual attractions to the leather goods more typically found in stables or on racetracks.

In fact, BDSM can exist without all of these external manifestations. It can quite happily play out between two people who are wearing jeans and T-shirts or who are doing something quite innocuous such as having lunch in a restaurant, and it need not require special implements or any proximity to a dungeon. It can be a way of life and it can actually go on ALL DAY!

For lifestyle BDSM folk it is as much, or more, about attitude than it is about activity.

And this is where it gets interesting.

A lot of the time the people who are more into the activity side of BDSM see it as primarily sexual. It often gets tied (no pun intended) to ideas of free sexual expression, libertarianism and then to gay-ism and lesbianism because these latter two isms, at least superficially for many people, seem concerned with what you do rather than the actuality of who you do it with.

This is perhaps a little unfortunate because having an interest in BDSM actually doesn't automatically switch your gender preferences around and make someone who once was straight, for example, into someone gay or bisexual the moment they pick up a flogger.

This jumbling of perceptions about BDSM creates a situation where we have people who care about BDSM and people who don't.

People who see BDSM in terms of sex or activities are often only temporary vistors to BDSM land. They see BDSM land as a sort of holiday resort where they can get a bit of slap and tickle, a bit of a laugh, a bit of grunting and then go home. At best they see it as a stamp in their passport of life experiences.

Lifestylers, on the other hand, live in BDSM land. They are residents. More to the point, because they live there they care about it a lot more than the occasional BDSM tourist. They care a lot more about how it is perceived by others and want it to be seen as a proper country rather than merely a destination for holiday rowdies.

This is a very different situation to the sexuality or gender-based lifestyle preferences made manifest when someone is homosexual, heterosexual or bisexual. No one is recreationally gay or lesbian, however you can be into recreational BDSM and not be a lifestyle BDSMer.

120

I certainly wouldn't expect people whose BDSM involvement is limited to occasional dalliances with fluffy handcuffs to become advocates for BDSM. I do wonder though, is there a point where people realise that for them BDSM is something to be taken more seriously than a sex aid or boredom alleviator, where it is not something which can simply be slipped back into a drawer until next time?

Week 31

Bumbling

Bumbling can be a defense mechanism.

Outside of BDSM bumbling can be cute or endearing. We might find someone appealing when they always manage to get lost when driving to somewhere, even to somewhere close. Or it might be endearing when they can't ever quite seem to get a cake to come out right, where their cakes always come out lopsided or not fully risen or where the icing always tastes a bit like fish. We might admire the enthusiasm of someone who makes furniture even though one side of whatever they make always seems higher than the other. We might know someone really means well when they go out to do some shopping, but they always manage to come home missing something even though they had a shopping list.

Inside of BDSM bumbling can be a defense mechanism. It can protect a dominant from getting too involved with a slave or a submissive. By being a bit of a bumbler the master induces the slave to not let down their own barriers completely or to not surrender completely because the slave sees that this potential master in front of them is getting some things right more by accident than design and thus is a risk. What if a circumstance arises where the slave needs the master to get it right and the master instead bumbles? It's safer for the slave if they keep their distance a little bit and don't hand over the crown jewels completely.

In a similar way a submissive or slave, when they're a bit of a bumbler, induces their master or dominant to keep their distance. After all, who wants to be the master of a train wreck which always seems just about to happen?

What I'm talking about here is how much we are prepared to commit ourselves to our partner. The more there is riding on someone's ability not to bumble, the higher the standard they need to achieve. Imagine having surgery done by a doctor who is known as a fine person with years of experience, who is highly knowledgeable and who 'mostly' gets it right. You don't wan't 'mostly'. 'Mostly' is not a good enough standard for a surgeon, and in BDSM it's not a good enough standard when you're laying your soul bare or where you're deliberately treading on very, very sensitive parts of someone's psyche.

When I talk about bumbling here I'm not arguing about being perfect, and nor do I want to suggest that having an absolutely complete skill set is a requirement for good BDSM. Making mistakes and being less than perfect are steps along the way to improving ourselves. They make us human and they help us connect with our also-human partners.

What I'm talking about are chronic bumblers, people who are bumblers by either conscious or unconscious design, who - in some way or another - choose to be bumblers.

There are reasons for making this choice. Amongst other things, bumbling can prevent uncomfortable intimacy. That doesn't mean physical or sexual intimacy because often there's a quite a lot of sexual intimacy involved in even the most cursory BDSM activities. Nor does it mean emotional intimacy because BDSM folk can get quite close through spending a lot of time together in challenging, demanding and highly-charged situations.

The sorts of intimacy which bumbling prevents are dominant intimacy and submissive intimacy. For dominants, it saves them from having to actually and fully master a slave. It avoids that type of closeness. A slave or submissive is always going to keep at least some distance in some areas when they are with a bumbling dominant and thus the dominant stays "safe".

Likewise, submissives and slaves can be sure that dominants will keep at least a little distance between themselves and what they see as potential train wrecks when they have to do with a bumbling submissive.

There are a lot of people who are eminently capable of rising above bumbling but who choose not to. They often have excellent-sounding reasons (read: excuses) for not doing so. A common one is the "it should come naturally" excuse. In this scenario, you don't have to study, you don't have to get training and you don't have to plan, *it should all come naturally*. And, of course, the end result is bumbling.

Bumbling is why some people don't have intense BDSM experiences. They may not realise it conciously, but when they're confronted by a partner who has consciously or unconsciously chosen not to improve their skills, knowledge or understanding, then they internally clam up and this makes intense experiences unlikely or simply impossible.

If someone doesn't have the skills now, doesn't have the knowledge now or doesn't have the awareness now but is keen to learn and is obviously working at it, then they're worth the investment of time and emotion. They're worth the investment of intimacy even if it's obvious that there will be a few bumps along the way. Someone who has chosen to remain static intends for there always to be bumps and always the same bumps. They're often not worth the time when you want more.

In a way I actually don't mind that there are bumblers. After people have met them, they appreciate me and my kind even more.

Week 32

The role of fear

I think that fear is not properly appreciated. It is an emotion to which many people have a knee-jerk, get-me-out-of-here reaction. Although it's not one of the feelings or emotions you can generally include in the warm-and-fuzzy category, it is one which we shouldn't ignore because it is a powerful emotion and this power means we can leverage it to create good outcomes.

One of the more frequent uses of fear in BDSM is the so-called mind fuck. Put bluntly, this involves using deception to instill fear or terror into a submissive while optimistically hoping that this fear or terror can be transmuted into arousal or excitement. I'm being mildly sarcastic in my tone here because mind fucks can actually work very well. One type of mind fuck, for example, is faux kidnapping where there are plenty of opportunities for blindfolds and bondage.

Fear is also a great tool to sharply focus one's mind. Some submissives can sort of fade out in the middle of scenes if things start to become a bit repetitive such as in a flogging. Pulling out a nasty-looking single-tail whip at such times, even if you don't intend to use it, is a good way to bring them back to the here and now.

Likewise, many submissives and bottoms will pay an awful lot of attention if they're tied, naked and spreadeagled, and you pull out a couple of scalpels or a pack of large-guage needles and announce that you're going to do some decorating on their skin, particularly if you hint that this might be your first time.

Another good thing about fear and terror are that they can induce the body to release adrenaline. This is a good thing in a scene because you generally don't want your submissive to nod off at some critical juncture. Adrenaline should nicely perk them up. Mentioning nipple play and then pulling out a pair of automobile jumper cables can also be effective here.

Sometimes I feel that there are too many rational, logical and reasonable submissives out there. If you want to get through this inconveniently sensible layer of their personalities and reach their primal cores (and who doesn't?), fear is an excellent way of doing this. Fear tends to wipe rational thought away and leave only the primal being behind. This is, of course, the being that's often exceptionally horny and which can't get enough of you. Any of the aforementioned fear-inducing strategies are quite fine for this.

A word of caution here before you start to think that fear and terror are universal panaceas for the times when it might seem that your flogger's batteries have gone flat or that your rope has become defective because neither appears to be inspiring the same ecstasy they used to. Too much fear and terror can lead to unfortunate conditioning where your submissive starts to quiver and quake (and not in a good way) when you enter the room. This is not desirable.

Fear needs to be cautiously, thoughtfully, safely and selectively applied so that it remains effective. Most of the time your partner should be fear-free because long-term feelings of fear do not transmute into arousal or excitement. They're just stressful. But, appropriately-applied, fear can be 'da bomb'!

Thanks for reading. To end this article, what else could I possibly say but:

Boo!

Week 33

The best service is the learn

I like service. I know that some dominants and masters are instead after partners to whom they can do evil things with rope, floggers, kitchen implements and whatever else comes to hand. Often this "doing" happens in the area between navel and thighs. Mighty orgasms and massive erections can be the order of the day for these folk and - let me be completely clear - I think that mighty orgasms and massive erections are very good things.

On the other hand, I like being served. Instead of me doing things to them, I like submissives and slaves who do things for and to me. If you happen to get off massaging feet then you're in luck with me because I happen to have two of them ready and waiting. If you delight in preparing fine repasts of lasagne then I may well be the dominant for you because my stomach can handle large quantities of it effortlessly. If you also seek a stern, determined and fair master who'll put you to good use then I'm very interested to receive your curriculum vitae.

Different dominants and masters have different desires and expectations of service. Some look for sexual or oral service.

Some look for housekeeping service. Some consider that being a willing bondage bunny or an ever ready target for a flogging or whipping is the ideal service.

I think that the best service of all is a dedication to learning, to never resting on your laurels, to always trying to discover something new. For me, having the service of someone who is static, who chooses not to grow, is uninteresting. In my own life I have chosen to keep learning, to always go exploring new things and to continuously develop my understanding of people, especially slaves and submissives. If I'm with a service-oriented slave who has decided they've learned enough then perhaps they will be satisfying today, but tomorrow I may well have outgrown them.

I think that for a submissive or slave learning comes down to three words:

1. Ask,

2. Study, and

3. Discuss.

Apply these three words generously in most, if not all, circumstances and situations.

It comes down to this:

If you do what I tell you then I will probably be satisfied. If you discover or develop some new way to serve me or please me then I will be delighted.

Week 34

Rules of service

When a dominant is trying to devise rules for their submissive, particularly at the beginning of a relationship, it can be a nightmare. Many dominants will want to lay down the law in fine detail and say things like, "You will always call me 'Sir'. You will aways have a journal entry ready for me to read by midnight every day. You will always be naked when I get home." And so the list goes on.

The problem with this level of detail is that there will frequently be situations where your submissive simply can't obey. For example, your inlaws may arrive unexpectedly and all four of you end up in the same room before you've had a chance to relax the "Sir" requirement. Your submissive might arrive home very late for some entirely legitimate reason and not be able to write their journal entry before midnight. Or the above mentioned inlaws might arrive just before you get home and your submissive can't be naked for your arrival.

Now some dominants recognise this and will modify these absolute commands of, "You will do XYZ", by adding exceptions or by saying, "Do your best." I don't like this because it makes orders rather rubbery. In my experience many submissives and slaves want and need to be bound by the orders they receive. They need to have the mindset that the orders are firm and are to be obeyed, not that orders possibly maybe should be obeyed if nothing gets in the way. By rubberising orders it makes obedience the exception rather than the rule.

On the other hand, some submissives and some dominants actually like it this rubbery way because disobedience can bring a reward. A slave may fail to obey an order for some trivial reason and say, "I am sooooo sorry, master. Let me bend over and pull down my panties so that you can spank me very, very hard!" Being able to slip up in the obedience department may be desirable so that there are excuses to engage in play punishment scenes.

This may work for some submissives and dominants. For service-oriented folk it's not going to be so successful. It weakens the experience for the submissive and can make it unsatisfying and unrewarding. The dominant can just find it frustrating.

Rather than focus on developing a finely-tuned set of absolute rules of behaviour which contain exceptions to handle every possible situation or difficulty I like the following five rules. Throw away any others rules you might have. Forget about ordering your submissive or slave to be naked when you get home. Discard telling them that they should always call you "Sir", "Master", "Lord", or whatever. With these five rules instead, a submissive should be able to work out what to do in most any situation:

1. You are serving me, not yourself. If your attention wavers or you neglect your service, I will frown upon this (where "frown" means apply some form of correction, possibly painful correction),

2. If an issue arises which affects, or has the potential to affect, the level of service I receive from you, bring it to my attention as soon as possible. If you do not, and particularly if the issue actually starts to affect your level of service, then I will frown upon this,

3. Communicate freely with me, but respectfully. Do not waste my time. Do not burden me with things which are not mine to bear. If you waste my time or burden me unnecessarily, I will frown upon this.

4. However, bring all issues which do require my attention to me promptly. Frowning will be the consequence if you do not. Not being sure whether something requires my attention is not an excuse (see next rule).

5. Learn. If you do not, I will frown upon this shortcoming. In particular, saying, "But I didn't know", when you could have asked is a very reliable way to earn a frowning.

The above rules are based on the idea that your submissive has a brain and is able to use it. I like these rules in part because they give your submissive an amount of responsibility for getting things right. Rather than having to memorise a detailed list of what to do and when, they can work it out themselves.

You can add detail where you feel it appropriate as a sort of addendum. For example, if you'd like a little bit more "Master" and less "Sir", you can say so and these fit into the operation of rule 5.

Instead of needing to order them to be naked when you come home, all you need to do is say that it pleases you when they are naked when you come home. Rule 1 comes into play here because in the ordinary course of events they'll be naked when you get home because that's the best service. If inlaws show up then it's obviously not serving you if your submissive strips off in front of them so they won't do it.

With only five short rules it's very simple, and simple is good.

Week 35

Why trying to fix a submissive is a bad idea

One of the troubling denizens of the BDSM world, but one who I have come to recognise, is the submissive who doesn't obey. I'm not talking about someone you meet somewhere and who simply shares your evil fascination with, say, rope, ice picks and anvils. Someone who is only your play partner in physical or sexual scenes is not someone I'd necessarily expect to be service oriented although they might be. After a particularly intense evening with the anvils and ice picks, when you're both exhausted, when there are pools of sweat everywhere and the air is filled with the smell of machine oil, then I'd think it's entirely reasonable for a purely physical partner to answer in response to an order to get you a glass of something cold from the fridge, "Piss off! Go and get it yourself, you lazy dominant!"

If you've got this arrangement to have a physical or sexual relationship in the dungeon, and you both are keen, willing and available, and if your dungeon times are intense, satisfying and leave your pink bits feeling like they need a holiday in the Bermudas, then the deal is satisfied. Both of you are getting what you want and agreed to.

On the other hand, the people I'm talking about here are the submissives or slaves who earnestly assure you that they'll be at your beck and call, who insists that they'll do whatever you want, and who claim loudly and repeatedly that they're only there to serve you. Then they don't and they aren't.

Actually, submissives who say they'll obey and who don't are part of a larger category of submissives who behave, for want of a better term, "poorly" on a persistent or repeating basis. Other behaviours in this category include:

- Being rude or disrespectful,

- Striking out verbally or physically,

- Being a smart-ass,

- Displaying a lack of concentration or lack of attention to detail,

- Losing interest rapidly in something they claim to be interested in or passionate about,

- Being a "good girl" or "good boy" when you're there and paying attention to them but not when you're absent,

- Displaying frequent attention-seeking behaviour, or

- Only doing well the things they want to do.

For the rest of this article though, and for simplicity, I'm just going to be referring to obedience, but any of the above can also apply.

So, getting back to obedience, what I'm saying is if someone signs up to be your submissive and part of the agreed deal is that they'll do certain tasks or be available in certain ways, then you can reasonably expect that they'll do these things. After all, they're an adult, right? They should know themselves and what they're capable of, right?

If they don't do what they say they'll do then:

1. They weren't serious in the first place and didn't mean what they said,

2. They don't know themselves and you can't trust what they say they'll do, or

3. While they may look like an adult, they're not.

Oddly though, many dominants and masters don't feel pissed off when it turns out their submissive won't or can't follow orders even though following orders was part of the deal.

I think there are a couple of reasons why dominants might behave this way. If this is all happening in an existing relationship which is moving into a BDSM phase then it might be that the dominant has made enough of an emotional commitment already that they are reluctant to risk messing it all up.

Another reason is that either consciously or unconsciously the dominant has acquired the idea that they, like Bob The Builder^{TM}, can fix it. If there's an issue with obedience, just as with any other issue in the submissive's life, why not simply give the appropriate orders and make the issue go away?

This doesn't work and can, in fact, be a trap.

I'd like to point out that the obedience problems I'm talking about are not one-off infractions like forgetting to buy the milk or slipping up on an item of protocol. What I'm talking about here are the chronic and repeated demonstrations of not following simple instructions such as always being late, always "forgetting" to do a particular task, and so on.

When the dominant steps forward and claims some sort of authority or responsibility for the lack of obedience by trying to solve it themselves, they can enable their submissive to continue the poor behaviour. What the dominant is actually doing is taking responsibility for solving the problem away from their submissive. The submissive then has less reason to try and fix their poor behaviour because it's not their responsibility any more. What we then have is a boundary problem as well as the original obedience problem.

We can see this sort of thing where a submissive is intentionally or accidentally disrespectful or rude to someone else and when they're challenged they say something like, "You have to take this up with my dominant. He's the one responsible for my behaviour."

There are some things which an individual - be they slave, submissive, dominant, master or vanilla - need to be able to do for themselves. These include being punctual, doing what they say they'll do, taking care of personal hygiene, feeding themselves, being respectful of others, etc. If someone told you that they couldn't feed themselves, even though they are physically and medically able to do so, because of "issues", then would you take over the responsibility and feed them? No, of course not. You'd encourage them to get professional help. If they claimed they were unable to wipe their own butt after a visit to the toilet due to "issues", would you reassure them and then take over the posterior-cleaning duties? No, also of course not.

140

While we might support someone, including our submissive, when they have problems - even if that problem is that they are a rude asshole - we can't and shouldn't take responsibility away from them. But some dominants try to do just that. When an issue appears - and everyone has at least some issues - then it can be oh-so-tempting for a dominant to step up and say, "Let me wield my mighty dominance and solve whatever problem you may have! I will say the magic words, issue a magic order and, 'Poof!', problem solved!"

If your submissive is chronically unable to do something, such as wipe their own butt (either physically or metaphorically) or follow orders, then they should get dismissed as your submissive. I mean, how awkward and embarrassing is it to be at a play party or some BDSM social event and introduce your slave to someone:

> "Hi. My name is Master SuperDude and this is my slave, scum-of-the-earth."

> "Greetings and salutations, SuperDude. My name is Roger The Dislodger. Tell me, what does your slave do for you?"

> "Well, she doesn't actually do anything. You see, she has problems with obedience..., but we're working on them."

> "How long has she had these problems with obeying?"

> "Ten years now, but we're nearly there."

And more than that, the original problem clearly isn't being solved.

That's not to say or suggest that these submissives are evil people who should be confined to BDSMer's hell where scenes stop just before they orgasm, where dungeon music is Barry Manilow singing "Copacabana" on repeat, where ropes are never quite long enough, where the tails of every flogger are irretrievably tangled, where the really good toys are either just out of reach or are in use by someone else, and where it's too cold. They may actually be a fine companion in some BDSM explorations and activities, but there are some important things to remember:

1. You're not their therapist. Don't try to be. You're their dominant. That's it.

2. If you try to fix them then you risk crossing the boundary between what's their responsibility and what's yours. You may play into their (unconscious) hands and reinforce inappropriate behaviour rather than correct it. You may become their enabler.

3. Provide opportunities to self-improve, but don't try to make your submissive take these opportunities - think horse, water, drink.

4. People don't behave poorly or inappropriately for no reason, and if it's well-entrenched behaviour then there are probably well-entrenched reasons for it to still be there. They may possibly be so well-entrenched that they've dropped below conscious awareness. Often poor behaviour requires the participation of a second person. Right now, this is probably you. You may become frustrated (and very confused) because your submissive might earnestly assert that they want to "get better" but nothing changes, no matter what you do. This may be because they're consciously, or more likely unconsciously playing a game with you - a game you didn't sign up for and don't understand.

The best thing you can do is have your own firm standards and boundaries. Discuss and support your partner (after all, your submissive is your partner here), but most importantly respect yourself, your standards and your boundaries.

Week 36

Just purpose

One of the items which I think every effective dominant should have is a sense of purpose. I realise that this isn't a "thing" which you can pack into your toy bag before you set off for an evening of delight and debauchery, but for many types of BDSM activities and relationships a solid sense of purpose needs to underlie them or else it all starts to feel a bit directionless.

Let me go back a step here and explain: Many slaves and submissives don't surrender themselves into the hands of their dominant just because of some physical or sexual activity at which this dominant excels. I know that bottoms do, that they'll often be interested in a particular top because of his or her skill in a particular activity - such as rope bondage or spanking - which happens to scratch a strong itch which that bottom has. For example, a bottom who finds that a hard spanking on a weekly basis is both very cathartic and gets their juices flowing is not going to be necessarily looking for domination on top of that. The spanking is satisfying on its own, thank you very much, and any further bowing, kneeling, worshipping or cooking of dinners is excess to requirements.

On the other hand, slaves and submissives are generally not looking for specific activities. Their want or need is going to be on the mental side of things. It's true that what happens between them and their dominant partner often plays out in physical ways - such as with the recreational inserting of bamboo under the fingernails or with water play by means of keelhauling, but the actual activities themselves are secondary to the psychological connection between the submissive and their partner.

Instead of surrendering to the actual physical play, sensations or pain as a bottom might do, a significant part of the surrender of a submissive is to their psychological interaction with their dominant or master.

What makes this interaction powerful and, in turn, the submissive's own surrender powerful, is the sense of purpose behind it on the part of the dominant. The more intensely the submissive feels or is aware of this purpose, this drive, this intensity of focus on the part of their dominant, the more profound their own experience is going to be regardless of whether it is experiencing being on the end of the lash, serving drinks, being manhandled, running errands or whatever.

A vital part of this is that the purpose is not only intense, but is just or right. The submissive needs to be able to get behind this purpose, to support it. If not, then some or all of the intensity behind it will be lost for them and they may only "go through the motions". Many slaves sign up to do whatever their master tells them to, but the amount of satisfaction they are going to get from serving is going to go down dramatically if they feel that what they're being told to do is unethical or unfair to someone.

So, a few important things come out of this:

1. As a dominant, you should have a sense of purpose. Where are you going with your submissive? What do you want to achieve with them? What do you want them to achieve for you?

2. Communicate this purpose to your submissive. Don't be vague with them. Make sure they're clear about where you want them to go. This helps them share the intensity.

3. You tell your submissive where you're going so they can surrender to the journey and work towards the destination with you. They need to have an overall confidence in this. That doesn't mean that you have to, or even should, tell them everything. They often simply need faith that you have them in hand, that you know where you're going and that it's a good place to go.

4. Having a purpose gives a dominant energy, a power which their submissive can feel.

You both will get more bang for your buck when that purpose is clear and your drive to get there is strong.

Week 37

The chocolate submissive test

Chocolate is an important tool for telling the difference between submissives. Especially when you're trying to work out what you can do with the quivering, eager creature before you, chocolate is easy to deploy and is pretty reliable.

Now, you could try tying up a submissive and see how they react. If they go all vague, their eyes glaze over or they get all squishy then you can tick the 'rope' box and prepare to move on to the next thing to try, maybe pulling the candles and the matches out of storage or polishing up the nipple clamps.

This process takes time because, of course, there are nearly a zillion different activities which you can test out on a submissive.

On the other hand, if you use chocolate you can exclude great swathes of activities in one fell swoop. This is what you do:

You put on your friendliest face. Make the submissive feel comfortable. Maybe be a little authoritative just to reassure them.

Then put a small block of chocolate in front of them and tell them to eat it. And watch.

You may only have a moment to catch this. Look for the hesitation.

If they take the chocolate and quickly gobble it up, and even when they say something like, "Your humble slave is SO grateful, master," then you've got a submissive who'll take all the good experiences you can dish out to them. Orgasms? They'll soak them up by the bucket-load. Floggings? Bring them on, gorilla arm! Bondage? They'll even bring the superglue and rope themselves!

On the other hand, if they hesitate, and especially if they momentarily look askance at you, then you've got someone who has serving you foremost in their mind. They don't want you to give them chocolate. They want to give YOU chocolate. They want to make you happy. They want to do things for you. They'll still eat the chocolate, but that's because you told them to.

And it only costs a few squares of chocolate!

Week 38

Slaves as labour-saving devices

I suppose that it's expected that we masters put our slaves to work for us. I mean, why have a slave if we can't get them to tote that barge and lift that bale? Aren't they there to do the "heavy lifting" in our lives? And, in fact, if we're doing our job properly shouldn't our slave be someone we see bowing under the pressure, who has sweat pouring from their fevered brow as we push them ever harder until we finally relent and let them fall to the floor begging for water and rest after we've drained them completely dry of energy. And then, once we're done, we look at this "puddle" on the floor, pat ourselves on our collective backs and think, "Good job!"

Of course this is the way things should be, isn't it?

I suppose the question actually should be: What is a slave? It can be a bit misleading, I think, to take the classical definition of a slave and apply it to the guys and girls we have at our feet. While we might be able to send our slave or submissive off to run errands, and having them in the house means that certain things are better managed, cleaner, tastier or neater than if we were left to do them ourselves, I'm not sure that it's actually a case of them being labour-saving devices.

Being a dominant or a master can be exceptionally cool. I know 'cos I am one. But it's not all beer and skittles. I think that our workload actually increases when we have a slave or submissive, however the nature of this additional workload is something we enjoy and find satisfying so that it can seem that we're working less because the work we're doing is a pleasure instead of a burden. And really, isn't this what we should all be doing - looking for work which we love?

This work of being a dominant involves planning, directing and, of course, dominating. Often there is a lot of focus and attention required. Good dungeon scenes don't just happen. Good discipline in the household doesn't just happen.

So, to answer my initial question: Yes, I think slaves and submissives are labour-saving devices and they can make life pretty cushy, but it's not a free ride. Maybe think of it like this: Slaves and submissives are like a pedal-powered toaster where you have to work for your toast.

I'm assuming, of course, that you like toast. I love mine with gobs of butter.

And with that imagery, I bid you adieu until next time.

Week 39

The right to inequality

I'm thinking of organising a march for the right to inequality.

Too long has society imposed on us a need to look at our partners, at our colleagues and at people we pass on the streets as equals. No more, I say!

When we pursue a master/slave relationship, society and the law expect and require that the slave takes responsibility for their actions. This can be in conflict with the goals of the master/slave relationship itself.

When someone is a slave, they can devote themselves towards serving the desires and whims of their master or mistress to the nth degree. Having to question what they're ordered to do to ensure that they don't cross any legal or moral line means that the slave necessarily takes back from their master some of the authority they have been working so hard to give.

For example, a master gives their slave a set of house keys and sends them to a particular address to bring back some documents lying on the dining room table. Doing this could amount to stealing if the owner of the house or apartment hadn't agreed to someone coming and taking those documents. In our present legal environment the slave could be charged with theft. If that happens then they might have a small amount of leeway in court if they claim ignorance, but the point is that they are exposed under the law. In an ideal world, if the nature of the master/slave relationship were recognised then the master would wear some or all of the responsibility in the eyes of the law. Obeying the orders of one's master would be recognised as justification.

There are precedents for one person having responsibility for the actions of another. In matters of business a member of staff following instructions from their manager to engage in some behaviour which places the business in financial or legal jeopardy is typically not going to be at risk. Instead, the manager is.

In the police or military, a subordinate following the orders of a superior officer is also not going to wear the consequences if things go pear-shaped.

In the military and in business, the responsibility for the consequences of a subordinate following orders falls on the shoulders of the person giving the orders. It's necessary for the operation of businesses and the military that this transfer of responsibility occurs. If it didn't we could get the absurd situation, for example, where a member of a road gang performing road works could be sued for damaging a water pipe when their supervisor or the person who planned the road works should take responsibility instead.

What we have here are hierarchies - in business, the military and elsewhere - and responsibility ripples up these hierarchies to the top and, as they say, the buck stops there.

When we're talking about master/slave relationships or dominant/submissive relationships we're again talking about hierarchies. These are hierarchies involving just two people. However, these are also hierarchies which society really doesn't recognise or understand. The same as with business or the military, the hierarchy is important to the well-functioning of the BDSM relationship. It's fundamental and for many of us folk the fact of this hierarchy is what we're looking for in the first place.

If we're seen by non-BDSMers as simply "kinky people" then the idea that there's a formal delegation or transfer of authority in our relationships is simply missed or not understood. In a business this transfer is actually expected and it's done by formally becoming an employee. In the police or military it is done by joining up and acquiring a rank. Society needs to learn, to be educated about us.

So, back to that march idea. Anyone care to join me? We can make a day of it. But, of course, be nice and don't annoy the police. If you get arrested, you're on your own... which is sort of the point, isn't it?

156

Week 40

Making *The Step*

Followers of my musings will be aware of my view that there are people who are merely occasional visitors to BDSM-land, and then there are people who either reside in BDSM-land or who are in BDSM-land so frequently that they may as well be granted full citizenship.

The occasional visitors are those people for whom BDSM and leather are simply kinky diversions. These are like the people who pass through on a tour bus which stops from time to time so they can all get out and take photographs or try a local dish before getting back in to move on to the next attraction.

The residents of BDSM-land aren't just there for the tour highlights. They're there for more subtle things, and they're comfortable and more than happy to be surrounded by, and immersed in, BDSM in all its glory and infamy.

How does one become a resident though?

I think that there's a step which needs to be made which moves a person from being an occasional tourist, a gawker or a member of the fluffy-pink-handcuffs brigade to someone who looks deeper, to someone who takes in more of what BDSM and leather have to offer than simply the hot stuff.

Not everyone takes this step of course, and I'll freely admit that there are many countries and places (both figurative and geographical) which I am more than happy to simply pass through because they're simply not what I want or need. But some do take this step and cease to be just a BDSM tourist or gawker.

I think this step has to do with surrender.

I think it has to do with an acceptance and the embracing of the realisation that life is significantly richer with BDSM in it, and significantly poorer without it. Kinky sex, fluffy handcuffs, and a bit of the ol' tying up are easy to do and equally easy to treat as superficial. Actually opening up and letting it all in to effect you deeply may not be a consideration... at least, not consciously. But for some people the pressure to open up is there. They may not recognise it initially, but they feel it and this surrender is not to some form of captivity or confinement, but instead is to release or liberation.

In some ways I suspect that this step is akin to crossing the threshold to adulthood, to becoming - if it doesn't sound too disagreeable - sensible.

It is making a profound commitment to a path, to an upcoming journey, one where we need to give of ourselves totally. I suppose it's similar to marriage, but instead of marrying a person, we marry the idea of being a leather person or a BDSM person. And it seems to be a till-death-us-do-part sort of thing.

The difference between someone before making *The Step* and after making *The Step* may not be obvious to those around them. They may continue to do the same things - tie the same knots, grovel on the floor the same way or wear latex which is just as shiny and colourful as before - but the difference is within. It is something internal and they may not even be aware of having made *The Step* themselves until something happens or someone says something and there's a click inside.

One day they think they're merely recreational bondage dudes and dudettes and the next day BDSM and leather are integral expressions of who they are. I think that for many it can be a great revelation which occurs in a metaphorical flash of light and a silent cry of, "It's all so clear now! Why didn't I realise this before?"

Hold on a moment... What was that?

I'll be right back. I think someone just turned on a light.

Week 41

There's sadism, and then there's sadism

The "SM" in "BDSM" refers to either "sadism" and "masochism", or to "sadomasochism", depending on who you talk to. I think it can be a point of pride for some people to be able to say that they're a sadist or even a "heavy masochist" when they're talking about their BDSM or leather pursuits. But are they really sadists? And are the "masochists" we see wandering around dungeons really masochists?

Well, no. Er... well, probably no.

You see, the point about sadists is that they get their rocks off by inflicting pain and suffering. At the end of a serious session with a victim, the common garden variety sadist would be revelling in the tormented, broken husk of a human they have brought into existence. In BDSM-land however, the outcome of a typical "sadism" session is a submissive, bottom or slave who is seriously sated, who feels some sort of resolution has been achieved and who has a feeling of intimate connection with their partner. This is exactly the opposite of what a real sadist looks for. A real sadist, if stuck with a BDSM submissive or bottom in a dungeon, would be infinitely frustrated and be forever crying out, "Stop having a good time!"

I suspect that there's a bit of linguistic convenience going on when we talk about "sadist", "sadism", "masochist" or "masochism". Externally, people who wear these labels in BDSM-land might look like they're going about their business doing the same sorts of things as everyday psychopaths, but what's happening internally is very different. In BDSM-land there's an almost explicit recognition that intense stimulation leads to profound satisfaction and if intense stimulation means strong pain, tight restraint or deep surrender and submission then so be it.

"Sadists" in BDSM can and do often use pain, torture, discipline and punishment with their partner, but the goal isn't to diminish the partner. It isn't to leave a whimpering shell as the end result, though this may be part of a larger process. No. The goal is to have a better, brighter, happier, more complete partner as an end result. Being "sadistic" in BDSM terms refers to making the partner more, not less.

Likewise, being a BDSM "masochist" usually isn't only about a bit of whacking followed by an orgasm. Nor is it about diminishing or degrading oneself. It's true that these two things can be part of a larger process, but BDSM masochism is really about growing. This isn't just personal growth, but also growing the intimacy and bonds in the relationship with your partner.

What we can observe is that for real sadists and real masochists the journey stops at the pain, the suffering and the submission. For BDSM folk this is where the journey actually begins. Everything up to this point for us is just packing the bags and getting ready to go.

162

When we look at pain, suffering, torture, surrender, submission, restraint and service, all of these important and vital words in BDSM-land represent departure points. They are the places from which we set off on our respective travels looking for surprise, excitement and self-discovery.

I don't actually like the way the words "sadist" and "masochist" are used in BDSM because they have dark and negative connotations while I find BDSM to be a bright, exciting and positive thing remarkably full of hope, promise and joy.

I suppose it doesn't help that we all tend to wear black, does it? Maybe bright yellow T-shirts are the way to go...

Week 42

Masters don't cry!

Trying to avoid showing any signs of weakness can be a strong temptation for a dominant. It's sort of implicit in the job title - "dominant" or "master" - that there's a certain amount of strength, fortitude or resilience involved in being one. But all strength has limits. All iron bars can be bent, so why hide the fact that this is so?

There are a number of reasons why a dominant might not want to put their limits on display:

1. Displaying limits has an impact on their ego and they think it makes them appear less dominant,

2. Because they're trying to maintain a fantasy-like image. This might be OK for a scene, or it may be dubiously acceptable when trying to make an impression at a party, but in a long-term relationship this doesn't fly,

3. Because their submissive leans on the image or illusion of strength and begins to feel uncomfortable when it's not there,

4. Because they feel like they're competing with other dominants (I know! This is probably a guy thing),

5. Because some submissives feel an overwhelming need to help and this can be annoying when you're sick or emotional and you just want a bit of quiet time to let healing happen naturally.

I suspect that number one (above) is the biggie, that in many cases dominants and masters avoid showing signs of weakness or vulnerability because they're afraid that it makes them less dominant: Masters don't cry. Masters are above such things.

This is crap.

The last time I looked, I was mortal. I am fairly sure that all the other masters and dominants I know are also mortal. We have feelings, we experience pain, we get headaches, we can stub our toes, we can sprain muscles and we can get indigestion. We're also emotional creatures - at times, anyway - and getting our feelings hurt or getting emotionally dented is just as likely for us when we open ourselves up to a partner as it is for any other mortal human.

There are differences in how we can react to pain and suffering though. If a slave or submissive is getting annoying we can despatch them to the farthest corner of our realm, then take deep breaths and calm down. If we happen to have our partner tied up we can create a bit of an escape by also blindfolding and gagging them. Slaves and submissives don't have this same luxury of escaping a master who is getting to be too much. If they can't use their slavish wiles to get a break, then they're stuck.

I think slaves and submissives often have to resign themselves to the fact that there isn't any escape. Maybe this surrender is part of the what they're looking for anyway. We dominants, on the other hand, can turn away and not show our feelings.

There's a limit to how much we can do this before not showing weakness becomes, itself, a weakness.

Being able to feel pain is not a weakness. I would even argue that a sensitive dominant - one who is vulnerable to pain and who is open to their own suffering - has greater potential as a dominant. They don't close themselves off from situations which are challenging or difficult and they are more likely to empathise. That's not a guarantee that they'd be any more dominant, but that there's definitely a better chance of a deep connection occurring with them than there would be with a dominant who simply "does" rather than "feels".

There are some times when it's definitely right to show weakness:

1. When you don't know something. Say "I don't know" rather than try to fake it. Faking it makes you look like a dick,

2. When you're sick or broken. Soldiering on when you've got a bad cold, food poisoning or when you've sprained something is not going to do anyone any good. You won't be able to concentrate and fully devote yourself to what you're doing with your partner - which is ripping them off - plus you can make yourself worse. It's better to say, "I'm sick", stop, and then come back another day,

3. Cry if you feel like it.

Trying not to show weaknesses or vulnerability is ultimately an act, quite literally. You're trying to act as if things are different than they really are. This can consume an awful lot of energy and become an intense burden in itself. It also distances you the most from the people you want to be closest to, such as your slave or submissive.

It's a burden I try not to carry. What about you?

Week 43

Avoided topics

This little essay came about because of my observation that people don't write about sex in personal ads.

This is, I think, an odd thing because couples do sex. Many people hook up and possibly within hours are doing the horizontal hula together. In fact they often get around to sexual explorations before they get to other nominal compatibility factors such as political leaning, education level, hobbies and so on.

Why don't people talk about sex in personal ads? Why don't personal ads say things like, "Must be intelligent, witty, professionally-employed and enjoy rutting like a priapic stallion?" Why are we so PC (politically correct) in ads? Why is sex *persona non grata*?

Here, undoubtedly, lies someone's university thesis.

More to the subject at hand though: Are things any different in the wildly wacky world of BDSM? Are there topics which we avoid discussing when we are considering compatibility with a potential dungeon partner?

On the one hand what we might call conventional or vanilla evaluation criteria apply - things like being intelligent, not hung up, gainfully employed, not living at home with parents, own car, attractive, not afraid of soap, familiar with deodorant, good sense of humour, similar political views, must not be vegetarian, and so on. I suppose that these are mostly very practical things having to do with spending lots of time together. These are all easy to talk about.

On the other hand there are the criteria which are relevant to BDSM - interest in bondage, dominant or submissive, pain enthusiast, into rough handling, curiosity about keel-hauling, well-insured, artistically creative in regards to wax and/or needles, own handcuffs, and so on. These are also easy to talk about.

So what isn't?

Well, sex is probably a good start. It always seems to be left as something implicit. I mean you might talk about dining preferences on a first date, even a first BDSM date, but who mentions having a propensity to insert alien objects where the Sun don't shine. Isn't it just as important? Well, maybe not in a cafe, but you get the idea.

People also don't seem to talk too much about looking for catharsis, even though it's quite common, or about having a desperate need to be helplessly crawling at someone's feet. Dominants and masters, when they're talking about finding a partner, might mention their skills with a flogger but rarely mention their own need to, say, inflict pain, see agony on their partner's face, taste blood, or smell their partner's fear.

I suspect that there are a few factors at play in regards to what we talk about and what we don't talk about:

170

- There's a desire not to seem vulnerable or weak, even though a lot of what partners find attractive in us is what we keep behind that very wall we try so hard not to drop,

- Though many BDSM activities, drives and desires are not what might be called socially acceptable, even within the BDSM community itself there are some things which other BDSM folk might find challenging to accept and saying that you're into them exposes you to the risk of being socially rejected, and

- Finally, I think that there's an element of social conditioning involved, a return of the idea of political correctness in that there are some things which we just don't talk about. It's not because we can't - it's because we learn that it's somehow not appropriate to do so and instead we hedge around the topic or make allusions. We might not even think of it at all because we have been so well conditioned.

I think that we do ourselves a disservice with this. We're not furthering our own cause of having useful, productive and satisfying relationships by hiding away things which are often very important to us. So I'd like to ask you: Are there things you don't talk about even though they are vital and necessary to what you need from your BDSM relationship? What is it that you'd like to be getting (or giving) but haven't pursued with your partner?

I'm feeling all inspired now. I think that the next time you see me I'm going to be wearing a T-shirt which simply says, "Woman! Assume the position! Panties optional." Do you think that would be too subtle? It's only a T-shirt after all.

Week 44

Maintaining mastery

For me, an important part of mastery is taking control. What I'm talking about is not where you simply tell a submissive or slave to go off and tote a barge or lift a bale. It's the actual exercise of the mental skills and abilities where you strategise, plan, analyse problems and come up with ways to achieve a particular goal.

Certainly it's very nice to have a slave bring you glasses of wine and pop grapes in your mouth while you, dressed in a roman toga and wearing a laurel head wreath, recline on a couch, and I would be first to say we masters absolutely deserve to be treated like this. But the big rush I get, the deep feeling of empowerment I get, comes from actually feeling control, using it, directing the flow and achieving change, making important moves towards a big goal or destination.

This goal can be something banal like solving a technical problem which has been bugging me for weeks, or it can be something much more interesting like finding a way to guide a slave or submissive past a mental obstacle or fear and see them blossom. The important thing about it is that I need to work for it. The mental sweat is part of it, knowing that I have worked, that I have pushed myself. It is about knowing that I have learned and grown, that this has made me a better dominant and has helped me acquire greater skills.

Part of it too is that it has helped me explore my own limits so I am more aware of where they are and thus I have a better idea of what I need to do to make me more capable, more skilled, and basically increase the territory over which I am able to roam.

The ability to do this is a skill in itself. Being ready and able to confront problems and find ways through or around them is something we learn and it is also something we can lose or forget.

This skill is vital for us as masters because one of the things our slaves and submissive look for is this same ability. Being able to tie a good knot or to gaze imperiously at a slave and cause them to wither before us are no doubt excellent skills, but once you've learned to do them are they then exercises in mastery, or do they become simply patterns of behaviour which we repeat over and over again?

In many cases it is the latter. Instead of growing, it becomes easier to repeat the things which we've done in the past. If they worked back then, why not use them again now?

What I'm trying to say here is that once you've learned to tie a knot, gaze imperiously or wield a mighty flogger then actually doing these things doesn't involve the mental skills you needed to learn them in the first place. The skills needed to learn and master these activities are the ones which make us good dominants and masters, not the actual knot-tying, imperious-gazing or flogging. I know many slaves and submissives who are extremely skilled with ropes, floggers, chains and you name it, but they're not masters and they'd never claim to be.

174

You see, the drive to dominate, to conquer, to control is often the thing to which slaves and submissives surrender.

The problem we masters have is that once we've learned to tie all the knots, and once we have learned to gaze imperiously in all compass directions, how do we keep our mental mastery muscles toned up and ready for action? If we don't need them so much because we've conquered most of the things we set out to do, what happens?

We can become mechanical masters following cookbook recipes of dominance simply because it's easy to do so.

To prevent this happening we might need to look outside of BDSM and leather. Those mastery skills we have aren't restricted to our BDSM and leather worlds. We can exercise them elsewhere and often it is simply a matter of confronting the new, the unusual and the strange.

This means not always following the cushy path. Look for other paths to follow, other things to learn and other challenges.

I have a guiding principle which I have been using for many years and it is that if something's new or strange and it is not going to kill me, then I am willing to try it. Rather than go hunting for the things I want to do, I let new activities and people find me and I try not to refuse when they appear on my horizon. You see, I've learned that when I go looking my choices come from what I already know and feel comfortable with. If the inspiration comes from other people or from other sources then it's not like that. I may end up hungry if a restaurant suggestion turns out to be some food which I don't like, or I may end up looking retarded if I try some activity for which I apparently have no aptitude, but by trying these things I also discover new things and have new challenges. This keeps my mental mastery muscles toned and ready for action.

Some days though, I do admit that I will go and see a brain-dead movie with no plot and zero chance of an Oscar (except possibly in special effects or makeup). If nothing else, every now and then a master needs some time off, doesn't he?

Week 45

Hedonism

I will admit to a tendency in my writing to focus on what some might call serious matters to do with BDSM - personal development, recognising the needs of yourself and your partner, communication, skills development, compatibility and so on. These are important in creating the well-rounded, happy and satisfied BDSMer.

I don't often write about hedonism though and I probably should.

I like hedonism, particularly in regards to myself. I like a bit of sensual self-indulgence. When we look at some of the things we do such as wax play, flogging and rope work, we can often recognise sensuality in them - a very raw, primal pursuit of physical or sexual sensual pleasure. It might well be that for some people there are other needs involved as well such as a need to serve, a need to experience control or a need for some form of catharsis, but sensual pleasure is very hard to avoid in many of the things we do in a dungeon.

Once we walk out of our dungeon it can be a very different story. This is when we often neglect the sensual pleasure side of BDSM.

I know that it's easy to think of sensual sexual or physical pleasure when you're somewhere where you can take off your clothes and rub, caress or fondle intimate body parts (preferably not your own), and I suppose it's also natural to turn off thoughts of pursuing this sort of pleasure when clothes go back on, but we don't need to.

BDSM is not just what what we do in the dungeon. For the folk who have dominant/submissive or master/slave relationships which continue outside of the dungeon, who live it in their day-to-day lives, it's important to remember that BDSM is a toolbox, a collection of things - attitudes, behaviours and activities - which we use to make ourselves happy and satisfied. It's something we can use to have a fucking awesome time just as much outside of the dungeon as in it. And I think we should.

You see, BDSM transforms hitting someone with a stick into impact play. It transforms verbally abusing someone into a humiliation scene. It transforms a flogging into a powerful experience of surrender. It transforms kneeling at someone's feet into awakening. In wax play it transforms inflicting superficial burns into sensual ecstasy.

Why can't it do this magic elsewhere as well?

Well, sometimes it does. BDSM can transform fetching someone a coffee into self-discovery. It can transform running an errand into a powerful feeling of being useful. These are both activities which non-BDSM people might find mundane but which become quite intense with BDSM.

BDSM has this ability to make something painful or even just plain normal into something wonderful and transformative. I think it's part of our job to look for this effect wherever we can and get the most out of our BDSM. I think we owe this to ourselves and to our partners.

178

Here's a list of things which are ordinarily sensual. My task then for you is to think about how BDSM can play a part in them:

- Dining out in a nice restaurant,

- Going for a walk in the sun or lying down in the sun,

- Horse-riding,

- Wearing clothes (hint: some clothes can feel sensual),

- Eating (or drinking) chocolate,

- Coffee,

- Having a hair cut,

- Getting a massage,

- Sailing, going for a boat ride or going for a ferry ride (consider rocking of the boat, sound of the waves, the wind),

- Listening to music,

- Bungee jumping,

- Parachuting,

- Scuba diving.

So, what sensuality are you going to look for today? Is pursuing hedonism on your list of things to do? How is BDSM going to play a part?

That's enough writing for now. In a little while my partner and I are going out specially to have lunch in Chinatown. I assure you that it's going to be fucking awesome.

180

Week 46

How much should you carry?

How much of your past experience with BDSM partners should you carry with you into a new relationship? The reason I ask is that I think that it's difficult to find a balance between cynicism related to partners who didn't work out, and uncontrolled optimism related to partners who did.

Many aspects of BDSM have to do with experience, skill and practise. We could talk about the physical skill involved when executing a bondage or flogging scene or we could talk about the learned ability to surrender fully and these are things which we can usefully develop and carry with us in all our BDSM dealings. But what we learn about people, what we learn from partners or potential partners is something which can colour potential new relationships. What we know, love or fear about people often affects our relationships with new people before we even actually meet them. Is this a good thing?

I suppose that if you're submissive and you learn that adopting certain postures, verbal mannerisms or wearing certain clothes gets the sort of reaction you want and need out of dominants who are right for you then this is a good thing. Such knowledge helps save time and prevents you accidentally pairing up with a dominant who may not do it for you. If a potential partner doesn't react "properly" then you can quickly cross them off your list and move on to the next one.

But there's a down side to this. What you've learned from past experience - both with yourself and with various dominants - lets you home in on what seems to be the right sort of dominant and, perhaps, in most cases this will work out. But at the same time this process also causes you to skip or neglect other dominants who may not match the pattern you've worked out but who may be an even better fit for you than the ones who do match your pattern.

The same sort of thing applies to dominants and masters. A brand new, straight-out-of-the-packet dominant isn't going to be very discriminating and will consider basically anyone who bows their head, wears a collar or acts even the tiniest bit submissively. They're initially going to have a tough time working out the sort of slave or submissive who is right for them but then they too will start pattern-matching based on experience. This is when they learn to separate the wheat from the chaff. Unfortunately, they too will then necessarily miss some of the wheat when they're discarding the chaff.

So, where's the balance point? How much should you rely on past experience when selecting or skipping a potential partner? Is it a matter of time? Are you in a rush to find the right partner and don't have time to consider possible maybes and can only spend time on yes definitelies? Or is it a matter of emotions? Is there too much of a risk of getting emotionally tied to someone who doesn't push the right BDSM buttons for you? Or are you concerned about the risk of being hurt too much?

182

Once we do start spending time with someone our past experience also affects how we behave towards them. Is it fair to behave towards a new partner in a way that is affected by experience with previous partners - good or bad? If, worst case scenario, a recent partner was an asshole, should we be defensive and behave as though our new partner might possibly be an asshole too? Or do we leave ourselves vulnerable to asshole behaviour and hope for the best?

I think it would be very nice if we could view each potential and actual partner with innocent eyes and not drag into the relationships the baggage from the past.

Where do we draw the line though? How much baggage do we bring with us? How much to we leave behind? Do we travel light with just a T-shirt, jeans and a change of underwear? Do we bring a whole wardrobe?

There are lots of questions today and I don't think there's a definitive answer for any of them because I think it is a matter of balance, a balance which each of us has to find for ourselves. What we can do though is raise this to consciousness, to think about it, to be aware of the choices that we make so that we can better guide ourselves to finding a right partner without carrying too much of a burden from the past. In a way this is actually mastery. It is choosing to master ourselves, to master the path we take and our choice of partner. And this sort of mastery is just as important for submissives and slaves as it is for masters and dominants.

Week 47

Effecting protocols

Protocols, simply put, are rules which tell us how to behave in particular circumstances. In diplomatic circles protocols determine how officials or representatives from one state or entity behave towards officials or representatives from another state or entity. Although it's not usually stated in the definition, these rules are intended to reflect how important these officials or representatives are supposed to be. For example, if you have the President Of Overunderland ('POO' for short) around to your palace for dinner and you serve takeaway pizza this is likely to offend because you clearly haven't put in much of an effort and that suggests you don't ascribe any value to their presidency.

There's an important distinction to recognise here and that is that the person is different to the office they hold. The actual person who is the POO may love pizza and be delighted to partake of a good four seasons, but when they're doing POO-related business activities then the office they hold is what everyone should be concerned with and everyone should act as if it has value - hence the protocols.

In many cases, protocols are designed to make absolutely sure that there is no doubt about the pecking order in a particular situation. Everyone's relative value is made glaringly obvious. This is why protocols contain rules about who speaks first, who sits first, who wears a hat and what sort, standard of dress, mode of speech, the giving of token gifts, the activities planned around an event, the food and drinks served and all stuff like that.

In short, protocols are about actively displaying a recognition of either someone's personal value or the value of the office they hold.

And now masters, dominants, slaves and submissives enter the picture...

Many of us are BDSM-monogamous. At any one time we would have only one single, important, one-on-one relationship with a partner. This is one where we recognise and engage this partner as a master, a slave, a dominant, a submissive or whatever. To us they are the full deal, the entire package, and we treat them that way.

It might well be that we meet other masters and slaves in our travels but often they're people we acknowledge more as fellow humans who share a common interest or passion. Although we might play or dally with these fellow travellers they don't get all of our masterly or slave attentions. We are to them, and they are to us, just ships which pass in the night and we pay attention to each other only fleetingly.

This means that we're not used to treating someone as just a slave or as just a master. Instead, we have a person who we might introduce to others as our master, our slave, our dominant or our submissive, but we tend to blur this office or role they have with the person themselves. It can be very difficult not to.

186

It'd be like a friend of the POO suddenly finding they have official business with the POO and struggling with protocol when, maybe even just the day before, the two of them were at a barbecue together sharing some prawns and a beer and having a laugh.

Although you might value your BDSM partner very highly as a person and comfortably treat them as a person, at times it's also appropriate to treat them in a way that is appropriate to the office and rank they hold. If they are your master then there have to be times when your behaviour, when the rules and protocol you follow, make evident that fact unequivocally. Likewise, when you have a slave or a submissive then there must be times when you treat them just like that. Your behaviour must reflect that they are your slave or submissive.

This is important because we BDSM folk are BDSM folk because vanilla relationships don't give us what we want, need or crave. If we allow the temptation to treat our partner as a person to win out too often then we start to find that either our own BDSM needs stop getting met or that we stop meeting the needs for which our BDSM partner became our partner.

A simple example of this can be when a top or dominant suddenly feels concern or compassion for a slave or submissive they are beating, supposedly mercilessly. This might be a very human reaction, but it's not what the slave needs.

Although we BDSM folk typically might talk about "high protocol" and "formal protocol", particularly when the topic of themed dinner parties come up, we also need to have our own protocols that make sure we don't drift too much vanilla-wards in our relationships. Recognising that someone holds the rank of master or slave in our lives means having protocols which guide our behaviour so that we show our respect for that rank.

Importantly, this is a way of keeping the BDSM alive between scenes or other planned activities.

The rules in your own personal protocols don't need to be nailed down as firmly as "high protocol", but at least think about what you do that shows that you consider and respect your partner as your slave or master just as much as you respect them as a person.

And speaking of nailing, I just remembered that I left my partner in the dungeon. I'd better go and let her down.

Week 48

Managing Oops

I guess it would quickly snap you out of a useful headspace if you were lying face down on a table having patterns carved into your back with a scalpel by your top and you suddenly hear them mutter a quiet "Oops!"

We'd all like to think and hope that each scene is going to go smoothly from start to finish and be completely "Oops"-free because when you're in the middle of a scene - especially when you're a bottom (but not always!) - it can be seriously distracting if you have to be concerned about what your partner is doing.

This is not always the case. Obviously, "Oops" moments are impossible to completely avoid and beyond the fact that they can instantly mess up a headspace that took a long time to get into, they also often mean that you have to stop and do something to un-"Oops" things.

Even if the "Oops" is not physically or medically catastrophic, such as one necessitating a visit to the hospital, there can still be a high price attached to it.

The price is low when there's not a lot riding on the scene. If you happen to live with your partner and have plenty of time for doing things together then a small "Oops" might just mean stop, apply a band-aid and try again tomorrow.

If there's a lot riding on a scene, such as when it involves two people who don't live together, where they don't have a lot of time together or where one or both might have been building up expectation for a week or more then the price of an "Oops" can be very, very high. In addition to a band-aid in such cases, expect much swearing and cursing to occur at a minimum.

Earlier I intimated that it's not just tops who can cause an "Oops" moment. A bottom who gets a cramp, for example, can cause an "Oops" and if, in a moment of wild agony or passion they scream out the name of their previous master or mistress, well… that's definitely an "Oops".

With experience you can anticipate many of the possible "Oops" incidents and plan for ways to mitigate them should they occur. An accidental wrap with a flogger can be an "Oops" event and recognising that it happened, apologising, and then pushing forward can be the best strategy.

"Oops" often means work. This idea is an important one to accept and embrace. It can be very tempting to try to metaphorically sweep an "Oops" under the bed, but the right thing to do is to deal fully with each and every "Oops" - even if it means putting your pants back on - so that you and your partner are free to move on to new and exciting activities without the spectre of past "Oops"s hanging over your head.

Especially recognise that the significance of what gets interrupted by an "Oops" may be very different for your partner than it is for you. What you might think as a minor inconvenience could be far more serious for your partner. Although I haven't mentioned it so far yet, communication is always going to be your best tool for making sure that an "Oops" gets well and truly un-"Oops"-ed. Talk with your partner and make sure that you understand both the gravity of the "Oops" situation *to them* and what's needed to fully and completely resolve it.

It's vital to have the real and certain expectation that each and every "Oops" is going to be dealt with properly and fully by you and your partner. In the face of certain knowledge that there will inevitably be "Oops" moments, the secure certainty that they will be handled, respected, and properly treated can ensure a good and productive headspace each and every time.

Week 49

Zoetrope - illusions of animation

I don't think it is unreasonable to "fake it" from time to time. There are bound to be times when a dominant/submissive couple are doing some shared activity and one of them is not feeling particularly involved but doesn't want to spoil the experience for their partner and so they adopt a sort of faux enthusiasm to keep things going.

I think that this sort of faking is acceptable for a few reasons:

1. It's temporary. It's a sort of bridge to span short, unavoidable periods of blah-ness,

2. Unless they're totally non-empathetic, the other partner usually knows that there's a lack of enthusiasm going on anyway, and

3. In most relationships there needs to be some level of give and take.

That's "most relationships" and it's worth reflecting on this idea of "most". In the spectrum of possible BDSM relationships we can argue that there's one type of relationship which might not need to have any faking at all and that's an owner/property relationship. In theory the person who is property has a completely utilitarian role - they're there to serve and to be useful and that's it. It's one way. Their role is like that of a table or chair. You shouldn't feel any obligation to sit on them to make them feel good. If you don't sit on them one day you shouldn't feel any need to make it up to them by sitting on them twice as much the next day, though if you do then we're not talking owner/property any more.

This short-term faking I'm talking about is something which probably falls under the heading of "relationship maintenance" or "partner maintenance". It's something which we all need to do regardless of which side of the dominant/submissive line we live on. It's part of what we contribute to a relationship. I know that "faking it" sounds a bit harsh, but I'm calling a spade a spade here.

What about longer-term faking it?

In the course of my travels I have come across many BDSM folk and couples who place serious demands on my imagination when they describe themselves as master/slave couples, or dominants, tops, submissives and so on. I watch them - not just for a couple of minutes but over months or even years - and find myself going, "Nope... Nah... Not happening... What are they thinking!?!?".

I'm sure that in some cases there are things I'm not seeing and that I am maybe completely wrong, but the phrase "topping from the bottom" is common in the BDSM world for a reason. It means that there are quite a few people who call themselves one thing but act like another. It's a bit of flimflam. It's an illusion.

I'm not sure how common or how extensive these BDSM illusions are. Some people, I know, simply play at BDSM and their plastic hand-cuffs and cheap floggers probably give them away. But they're playing at it and make no pretense to be doing otherwise. They flirt with something which many others of us find quite profound and that's OK. Not everyone needs to be on the same ride.

But others seem to seriously devote themselves to creating and maintaining a BDSM illusion. They learn and replicate some of the "moves" of a particular role. It's easy, for example, to dress in the style of some masters, to grow a masterly moustache, to pick up a few masterly phrases and learn how to stand and move like a master. These don't make you a master. Likewise, there are moves which slaves and submissives make which are easy to learn like some forms of bowing and kneeling. But it isn't the moves which make the person, it is what's behind the moves. It's what the person feels, what motivates them, what drives them. These are what make a master or a slave, a dominant or a submissive, a top or a bottom.

I think that there are many reasons for creating an illusion of BDSM:

1. Wanting to get one's end wet (or some other benefit),

2. Hoping to grow into the role: If I act like a dominant or a submissive then maybe I'll become one,

3. Insecurity - needing to fit the role because you think it's expected or that you'll disappoint your partner if you don't,

4. Lack of awareness - not knowing any different or not realising that it's possibly harmful,

5. Wanting more out of BDSM, but being afraid to go for it for real,

195

6. Wanting to get and keep a particular partner or a particular type of partner.

The title of this article is "Zoetrope - illusion of animation". This is because the zoetrope is an old-fashioned, simple device which presents a repeated sequence of pictures of an object in such a way that our brain sees the object as being in motion rather than being simply a series of "stills". The BDSM illusions some people create are exactly like that. They create a series of snapshots - words or actions - and think that if they present them smoothly enough that they can fool others (and maybe even themselves) into thinking that what's there is a real BDSM master, slave, dominant or submissive.

I think that maybe we can draw a line that helps us determine the difference between reality and these illusions. It comes down to this: Is what we're seeing a reflection of what the person actually feels, or is it a reflection of what they would like us to see? Are we seeing a zoetrope, or are we seeing reality? If all we see are the same images or snapshots, or the same words or actions, repeated over and over again then maybe it is just an illusion of animation, a carefully curated subset of behaviours that the person would like us to see and then think that they are the real deal.

These same images or behaviours which get replayed over and over again occur because there's no new material available. The illusionist can copy what they've seen before but because they don't actually feel it themselves they may not be able to create anything new and original.

Now it's quite possible that for some people the snapshots are quite sufficient. Maybe it's like the tourists you see who are so intent on taking pictures of where they are that they don't stop to smell the metaphorical roses. Maybe it is enough for some to merely look the part of a BDSM master or slave.

196

For me though, the reality is far more important that the image. I sometimes joke in my writing about the BDSM master who wears a straw hat and a Hawaiian shirt. To me this is an anti-master image and I think the contrast is funny, but I also think if I ever meet one at a play party then he'd have to be either a dickhead of the highest order or else a master who has the goods, who knows it and who doesn't need to present an image or an illusion.

So, if you see a guy at a play party and he looks completely out of place because he's wearing a straw hat and a Hawaiian shirt, and especially if his name tag says "Peter Masters", be open to the possibility that he's a master *par excellence*. Either that, or he's being a real dick. There's a good chance either way, really.

Week 50

Because you say I can

I dominate you because you say that I can. This is the idea of consent. Of course, consent can be a very nebulous area and the most treasured variety of consent, namely fully-informed consent, can be hard to come by because it requires an awful lot of experience[1] plus study to actually reach the point where you are fully informed.

But what actually happens in a wider sense when you or I consent to engage in some BDSM activity or relationship?

Let's start by considering an encounter at a play party. Maybe two people who don't know each other - a dominant and a submissive - meet up, start chatting and realise that they have complementary animalistic urges. They agree that the next step might be finding a quiet room, unpacking the dominant's toybag and proceeding towards some, er, mutual stimulation.

---

[1]Rather than a lot of awful experience... but then again maybe not.

Anyway, the point is that they've talked and they've agreed on what they're going to do.

Each of them has also implicitly decided to commit resources to this activity, resources that they can't easily recover if the agreed-upon activity goes south. This is because when you go to a play party you often only have one shot at doing something serious with someone. Certainly if you're only talking about a few knots or a few quick taps of a cane then you can easily do multiple light scenes in an evening. But unless you have a lot of experience it's hard to mentally rewind and start again with someone new if a more serious scene gets aborted such as a complex suspension bondage or military interrogation scene. And if it was a heavy impact play scene that didn't work out then the fresh canvas of your unbruised body might not be available again for a couple of weeks.

The thing is that negotiation and consent almost always mean that both people involved are going to be committing time, energy, emotions or their bodies. And they're probably consciously or unconsciously hoping for some return on this investment.

This is starting to sound like a sort of contract. When you enter into a contract with someone you spell out what each party to the contract puts in to it and what each gets out of it. When we talk about contracts there's also the explicit idea that we're talking about two people.

When we talk about consent in BDSM the understanding is more that it's about one person - often a submissive or bottom. In reality, of course, there's a dominant or top involved too, and the dominant or top is going to have their own expectations of what they want or need to get out of the scene or relationship once there's been consent. They're not going to be devoting time and effort for zero return.

Even the heroic dominants and submissives who actually put themselves in the firing line for disappointment when they volunteer to play with or teach newbies are doing so because they find it rewarding.

Probably the biggest disappointment though is when they give their time to someone who doesn't take it seriously.

It's not always going to be the case that a scene or even a relationship pans out. There can be entirely legitimate reasons why a scene is cut short such as a cramp, illness or some unavoidable outside disturbance and this is just life. Relationships also sometimes don't work out despite best intentions.

I think my point is that even when we're not talking about a contract, anything we consent to or agree to - whether we do it as a top, bottom, master, slave, dominant or submissive - is going to create expectations or hopes in our partner. This is the case even for a casual partner. And they're going to commit their time and energy based on that agreement.

It's something we shouldn't take lightly.

Week 51

The allure of flogging

If there were a competition for the most popular BDSM dungeon activity, I think it would be a two-horse race between bondage and flogging with the result probably being a tie (Haha! OK. Sorry. Obvious joke.).

If we put bondage to one side, why is flogging so popular?

I think that part of it is because there's an image associated with flogging. It's an image of someone naked with their hands tied above their heads to a bolt on a bare stone wall, being whipped and flogged mercilessly by their evil captor and with blood and sweat mixing in pools on the floor beneath them as they writhe and howl in agony. This is, of course, terribly sexy.

Secondly, it can be deceptively easy to get into flogging... on the business end, anyway. Floggers can appear harmless. Someone cautious about getting into BDSM for the first time can be shown a lovely, soft, decorated flogger and they'll think, "Well, what possible harm could that do?"

Thirdly, there is an enormous variety of floggers available. They can be made of various types of leather, rubber, string, hair and most anything else that's long, thin and flexible. They come in a wide range of colours and styles. As well as allowing the dominant a lot of control over the range of sensations or pain they inflict, floggers are, in fact, almost perfect for shopaholics.

Fourthly, floggers can be applied in an infinite number of ways. A dominant can use a flogger and strike hard, soft, slow or fast. They can hit on the back or on the buttocks, and a light flogger can be used on the chest or on the pink bits further down. If the dominant turns the flogger around they can also insert it handle first.

Fifthly, floggers are good exercise. Many tops and dominants are almost constantly served hand and foot by their submissives or slaves and it is only flogging which staves off indolence and an early grave due to inactivity. Indeed, dominants can have quite massive biceps precisely because of the workout they get from flogging.

And, to add a slightly more serious tone, floggers are tools of control, and control is the name of the game for many dominant/submissive couples. Flogging can be sensual, sexual or painful. It can be physically aggressive and rough or it can be light and gentle. We could maybe compare flogging to playing a musical instrument like the violin. The violinist is the dominant, the submissive is the violin, and the flogger is the bow. The dominant "plays" the submissive using the flogger. The more skilled the dominant and the more familiar they are with their instrument the more they can get out of it.

We might be tempted to see flogging as one person making another person really horny or giving them orgasms, but I think the best tops and dominants do much more than that. Lots of people can play "Fur Elise" on the piano and make it sound passable, for

204

example, but it's obvious when someone with real skill plays it even though they play exactly the same notes as everyone else.

I've always thought that there's a lot of creativity possible in flogging, a lot of artistry. Much of it is due, I think, to the flexibility of a flogger allowing the dominant to inflict exactly what he or she wants, when they want and where they want. In doing so it allows the artist in the dominant to fly free. The submissive or bottom is the instrument. They surrender to this and a flogger allows their dominant free reign to play them.

This is how it should be.

Week 52

Looking for a master

Dear valued customer,

Thank you for contacting Masters-R-Us and enquiring about our range of masters.

At the moment we are well-stocked with the Mighty Master Man which has a pull-string on the back. Pull the ring attached to the string and he speaks! Among the phrases he can say are:

- Kneel, bitch!

- Bring me my flogger!

- What a lovely arse!

- Adopt the position!

- Oops. Sorry. I didn't mean to hit there.

- Is it supposed to look like that?

- I didn't think that was supposed to happen.

- When is it my turn?

- Sorry about that. I'll buy you a new one first thing tomorrow.

- Oh. I know why it's dark - it's you who is supposed to wear the blindfold!

- Hold this for a moment.

- I promise you that I really do know how to tie knots.

- I washed it and it shrunk.

- I used to have one but they took it away as evidence in a police enquiry.

The Mighty Master Man is available in two models. The Action Master has a real black leather cap and vest and real black leather chaps. The Holiday Master has a Hawaiian shirt, straw beach hat, shorts and sandals. Each comes with a colour-coordinated flogger.

When shopping around for a master keep in mind that they don't make masters like they used to. It's well known that the older masters last much longer than the newer ones. And when you're trying to work out which buttons to push to get what you want, with the newer ones you often only get instructions in some language which seems like it might be English but it's been translated from Swahili by someone with a cheap dictionary or who has only read the Dummy's Guide to Domination and who was in a hurry to go home for the day.

A useful master should also have an off switch. Often they just want attention at all the wrong times and it's good if you can turn them off. Otherwise they can be like the Energiser Bunny and you have to put them in some corner and let them bang their little cymbals or wave their little floggers until their get up and go has got up and went.

When you're really feeling driven to find a master, you may be tempted to consider bait to trap one. I won't say the obvious remark about master baiting, but as long as you're looking for a master who is a dude then tits are pretty much all you need. Master dudes are quite simple that way. Quality can be quite variable if you trap one and I would recommend sticking with an emporium such as our own which has a proven track record.

With persistence you can be lucky. When you find the right master it's like finding the toy you were really, really, really hoping to find in that packet of cornflakes. It's Christmas in your underwear!

If you have any further questions or if we can be of further assistance, please don't hesitate to call or write. Further details on our range can be found in our online catalogue at http://www.masters-r-us.com/

Yours,

Peter Masters